GOOD MARRIAGES GROW!

GOOD MARRIAGES GROW!

A BOOK FOR WIVES

by

Irene Burk Harrell

WORD BOOKS, Publishers

WACO, TEXAS   LONDON, ENGLAND

Grateful acknowledgment is made to the following for the use of copyright material:

CHRISTIAN LIFE MAGAZINE
Article entitled "Merry-go-round Miracle," copyright August, 1967, Christian Life Publications, Inc., Gundersen Drive and Schmale Road, Wheaton, Illinois, 60187. Used by permission.

CHRISTIAN WRITER AND EDITOR
Article entitled "My Kids Help Me Write," *Christian Writer and Editor,* copyright Winter, 1967, Christian Life Publications, Inc., Gundersen Drive and Schmale Road, Wheaton, Illinois, 60187. Used by permission.

CHRISTIAN BOARD OF PUBLICATION
Article entitled "TV Or Not TV," from *Hearthstone.* Published by the Christian Board of Publication, St. Louis, Missouri. Used by permission.

BOARD OF PUBLICATION OF THE EVANGELICAL UNITED BRETHREN CHURCH
Quotations from "Our Expecting Family," from *Church and Home,* Used by permission.

LITTLE BROWN & CO.
Poem entitled, "A Word to Husbands," by Ogden Nash. From *Marriage Lines* by Ogden Nash, copyright © 1962, by Ogden Nash. Used by permission.

THE SUNDAY SCHOOL BOARD OF THE SOUTHERN BAPTIST CONVENTION
Quotations from "Schedules For Family Living," "Good Marriages Grow," "Getting 'It' Done," "Too Much Togetherness," from *Home Life.* Used by permission.

DAVID C. COOK PUBLISHING CO.
Article "Seeing Stars" reprinted by permission from *Sunday Digest,* © 1967, David C. Cook Publishing Co., Elgin, Illinois.

THE METHODIST PUBLISHING HOUSE
Article "Every Child Should Be an Only Child—Once in a While" reprinted by permission from *The Christian Home* © 1968

MOTHERS' MANUAL, INC.
Quotations from "Our Fifth Baby" reprinted by permission from *Mothers' Manual,* © 1965.

Library of Congress Catalog Card Number—68—31112

Printed in the United States of America

For Allen and the kids—

bless 'em

Foreword

I was rereading this manuscript one afternoon, putting the finishing touches on it before sending it to my publisher, when my oldest son came in and looked over my shoulder. He laughed, pointing to the typewritten title page lying in front of me.

"That looks like *Good Marriages Growl*," he said.

Sure enough, the exclamation mark at the end of the title could be mistaken, from his vantage point, for the letter "l".

I guess our marriage *had* growled a lot—not that my husband and I had ever growled aloud at each other, but there had been growls just the same. We know that God has used even the growls to help our marriage grow to what it was meant to be. And so we cannot choose to erase even the unlovely parts.

In the first paragraph of the first chapter I'd acknowledged that our marriage might have been happy *because* of our imperfections. That proved to be truer than I'd realized.

Recently a clear understanding of our own miserable imperfections had brought us to a full surrender to God in a way that none of our alleged virtues ever could. And so we must thank God for our faults.

Good Marriages Grow? They *have* to, all along the way.

Here, then, is a random sampling of some of the happenings—serious and frivolous, spiritual and otherwise—along the way as our good marriage grew. That it still needs to grow, and that it has been woefully immature at some places, will be abundantly clear to you.

Many of the solutions I've proposed here to family problems, to problems with children and spouses, seem trivial to me now, and quite beside the point. There is only one Answer to all our problems: complete commitment to Him and His purpose for our lives, so that our very problems become His to solve as we lift them up in prayer. But before we were able to receive that Answer, there were some techniques and common sense solutions that seemed useful. They helped preserve us on our way to His Way. And so we want to share them with you.

Christian living is not an accomplished state but a growing process. We haven't been perfect all our lives, or even reasonably intelligent. We're still not. But God has brought us a long way from where we started. Our prayer is that some of what we've learned along the way may communicate itself to you in these pages; that it may help you to survive until the day when you and your husband or wife are ready to get on your knees together and begin to live.

Most of the chapters in this book have already been published as articles in magazines. I am grateful to the publishers for their permission to reprint the material in this collection.

IRENE BURK HARRELL
September 4, 1967

Contents

GOOD MARRIAGES GROW!

1

Good Marriages Grow

MY HUSBAND isn't perfect—thank goodness! If he were, I'd feel horribly guilty about saddling him with me. I seem to have missed perfection by a few billion light years myself. But, together, we've had an unbelievably happy marriage for almost fifteen years now, in spite of our imperfections—or was it because of them?

Looking back, thinking about all the days of our lives together, I can see some of the reasons our marriage succeeded, while others, apparently more promising, failed somewhere along the way.

Our beginnings were certainly not auspicious. Our backgrounds were quite dissimilar. If we hadn't both found ourselves attending the same university we'd probably never have met. As it was, I almost didn't go to the dormitory dance where we introduced ourselves.

But the "I'll-go-down-if-you-will" dares of roommates persuaded me to put on a long black dress and enter the big parlor. I didn't dream that three and a half years later I'd be entering the same parlor, in a long white dress, ready to say "I do" to a boy just then summoning the courage to ask me for a dance.

I didn't think he danced very well, but then, neither did I, so we stepped on each other's feet for a while before we sat down to discuss world affairs. With the omniscience of youth we knew more answers then than we've ever been sure of since.

I was a nearly city-bred Yankee and he was the son of a southern tobacco farmer. I didn't even believe in smoking! Our college dating covered a brief four months after which I returned to a northern library to work while he finished his schooling down South.

Our letters to one another were long, frequent, and affectionate at first. Then they dwindled to occasional short, polite, little notes as both of us were busy and involved in dating other people.

We occasionally reminisced about our idyllic times together in Chapel Hill, however, and two years later he invited me South for a college weekend. It was a lovely one, but heartbreaking to me because I had grown up enough to realize what a prize he was— and he didn't repeat the proposal I'd rejected two years before.

I went home sadder and wiser, not realizing that his interest in me had been rekindled too. Our expenditures for postage increased. There were dizzying ups and downs before we finally decided to join our lives a year later, after many postage stamps had been licked and stuck on upside down.

After our engagement I met my future father-in-law. It was obvious that he thought his son had made a bad choice. When I visited his home for a weekend he had almost nothing to say. Then, the day I left, he offered a laconic parting remark.

"Well, you've been," he said. "If you can stand us, you're welcome to come back."

He's told me since that he thought that was the safest invitation he'd ever issued. He was sure I'd never meet the qualification.

He laughs now, reminding me of it. "Never been more wrong about anything!" he chortles when he comes to see us. "Why, you've turned out to be the *marriedest* pair I've ever seen!"

It's a good thing too. We're responsible for five of his grandchildren.

How did it happen? Was my father-in-law wrong in his first judgment of me? In a way, he was. But in another sense he wasn't wrong at all.

The person I was *then* could never have been a good wife for the boy whose ring I wore. And he wouldn't have been the right husband for me. But we never had to find that out. Because we changed, all along.

Like other good marriages, ours was not ready-made, it grew. And we grew with it, changing from what we were then into what we are now. And we don't for a minute deceive ourselves into thinking that the need for change and growth is over. Instead we are both looking forward to what comes next.

We're beginning to understand the poet's lines about "the best is yet to be, the last of life, for which the first was made."

2

His Folks—And Yours

WHAT ABOUT marriages that fail to grow into good ones?

As judge of a city court, my husband has daily contact with them. Spouses in court to get their "rights" fit into a pattern of "wrongs" in their relationships. Our own experience in living together has shown us that good things can come from the very areas that often spell "trouble."

Some of the most common problems leading formerly "courting" couples to court are those involving in-laws. Most in-law jokes have an unhappy basis in fact.

Here, we were just plain lucky. My folks were six hundred miles away—too far for interfering even if they'd been inclined to bother us, which they weren't.

Allen's parents were just a few hours away by car. But not once did they offer to intervene in our affairs, even when they must have felt that some of the things we were doing were either unwise or foolish. My mother-in-law was blessed with such uncommon good sense that she wouldn't even give advice when I asked for it.

"Well, it'll be whatever you decide," she used to say. "You're the ones who have to live by what you choose."

How helpful that was! It meant that our mistakes and successes were always our own, with all the credit or blame for ourselves.

I wince whenever I hear of a newly married couple beginning their lives together as guests in the house of her parents or his. Being a good wife or husband is quite different from being a good son or daughter. At the very beginning of married life the two roles are bound to be incompatible, especially if each is expected to be a twenty-four hour a day occupation. If a young couple, very much in love and eager to marry, can't afford to live apart from their parents, I always say, "Wait."

One girl of my acquaintance decided she knew better. Her mother-in-law was, she told me, extremely fond of her and very easy to get along with. She was sure they could live together in peace and harmony.

They lived together all right—very much together—about as together as they could get. There was not even a door on the newlyweds' bedroom, only a skimpy curtain hung in the doorway, and Mama-in-law slept directly across the hall.

Their love may have been blind, but it could not comfortably assume that the rest of the household was not only blind but deaf and dumb as well. Their necessity for only circumspect behavior stifled the spontaneity that nature sometimes insists on.

Well, that marriage is still intact, but the mother-in-law-daughter-in-law relationship is far from lovely. And the marriage didn't get off to a strong and happy start.

In our letters to one another before our marriage, Allen and I discussed the possibility of living with his parents. We'd have been welcomed there, and he'd have had a good summer job working on the farm. We certainly could have used the financial benefits.

But I've always been thankful that circumstances combined to make us rent a tiny, barely furnished, on-campus apartment for an exorbitant rent of something like eighty dollars a month. We had a living room, a bedroom-dining room combination and a kitchen so tiny that when I spilled a cup of milk I had to mop the entire floor. We shared a bath with a girl in an adjoining apartment.

The rent was outrageous—we could have been buying a house

for less—but we were too much in love to know that. Besides, we
thought the built-in bookcases in the living room were "cute."

I could never seek out advice or sympathy from my parents nor
could Allen from his. Although we made many big and little mistakes that way, we didn't have an opportunity to make the biggest
mistake of all—that of "telling on" each other to outsiders.

It seems to me that a near-perfect rule to follow about the telling
of your marital woes (and everyone's bound to have *some*, especially
at the beginning) is to discuss them only with someone who will
send you a bill for listening. That limits it to professional advice-
givers—lawyers, counselors, doctors—who might actually be able
to help, not to someone who'll convey your disgruntlements to the
neighborhood and so wear away all the important faithfulness
and loyalty a marriage must have.

3

Dollars and Sense

A LOT OF marriages have trouble about money. We haven't yet. That may be because we've never had enough money to argue about. Our creditors have always decided for us where our money had to go if we wanted to keep on eating bread and wearing shoes.

Our relative poverty, sufficiently acute to keep me out of beauty parlors and dress shops, was certainly beneficial to us. I never pretended to keep up with the latest styles.

It's a good thing it didn't matter to me that we couldn't afford beauty parlors. My hair, originally straighter than broom straw, actually began to curl a little when my premarital permanent left it and was not replaced by a new one.

Now when people say to me, "Gee, but it must be nice not to have to curl your hair," I smile graciously—I hope. I don't bother to explain that theirs might wave a little too if they were too broke to go to the beauty parlor and too busy to do any fixing of it themselves. They'd never believe me. I'd not have believed it either, but that's exactly how it happened. Sometimes hair curls because of the shape of the hair follicle—other times it curls in self-defense. And the results are practically indistinguishable.

It's no wonder that husbands get unhappy and marriages have troubles over women's fashions in coiffures and clothing. Think about it. Don't most of our fashions make sense to a man only if he happens to be a designer or a corset-fitter or a chiropodist or a hairdresser or a backache man or a psychiatrist or a banker or a flooring manufacturer or an eye-ear-nose-and-throat fellow? Then they make sense only because they mean dollars to him.

If, however, all he is is a husband, especially a financially insecure one, that's a different matter. Have pity! Have mercy! And look at it the way he does.

For instance? Well, hats, for instance. They never keep a head warm—except when your husband gets hotheaded over the bill. Most of 'em seem to be designed to give a stiff neck to any husband unfortunate enough to get pewed behind one in church. It doesn't help to ask the lady to please remove her hat. She might do it, and SPRONG!!!—out would pop a coiffure that would astound a Fiji Islander! Then even the man sitting *beside* her can't see the preacher!

A man used to be able to expect just plain hair to be under a hat. That was before bleaching, darkening, curling, straightening, teasing, and permanents made hair more temporary than nature intended. Now he has to buy you a wig!

Modern hair fashions are not only slow murder to the hair and expensive to maintain; they are also impossible to caress without danger to the caresser, and they're a perfect fright to go to bed with at night. They're bound to be about as uncomfortable to sleep *with* as to sleep *on*. No wonder the divorce rate keeps going up.

Our hairdos outdo the postal service in their imperviousness to the elements. Neither snow nor rain nor heat nor gloom of night (nor impassioned spouse) strays a hair from a modernly coiffured wife, all lacquered and sprayed. DO NOT TOUCH—but here's the bill. Should we be surprised when husbands contemplate the joys of bachelorhood?

And faces? They're covered with such sensitive skin—not because they were born that way, but because they have had to suffer such an unbelievable conglomeration of ingredients and exposures to make them look like what they're not. The expense—

in time, inconvenience, unrecognizability, and money—of putting on a face has increased to the point where I understand some husbands are going to start agitating for the "faceless" look next season. Can't say that I blame them. It's bound to be an improvement.

Lobes of ears, next on the agenda (you can hardly call it a human form any more), used to be delicate and *so* inspiring. After the ravages of heavy junkyard jewelry, our earlobes are still inspiring. Only instead of inspiring something like tender romance they remind your husband he forgot to pick up the cubed steak at the butcher's.

Necks were, for a season, forgotten under tons of turn-your-neck-green jewelry. Some recent neck-nuzzling I heard about advertised itself with two chipped incisors and a nose that looked tarnished for a week.

Torsos? Ah, now there's something your husband could sink his teeth into—or could in the good old days when nothing more formidable than a framework of steel stays stood between him and the softness of his beloved. But fashions aren't what they were, and these days, an amorous mate is likely to get a mouthful of asbestos or steel coil or sponge rubber or some utterly unidentifiable synthetic (indigestible too!) if he depends upon your "ouch" to curb his playfulness. Seems like he doesn't reach you any more? No wonder.

Husbands' feelings about the fashions we are forced to wear on our legs are too strong to be expressed in a book as polite as this one. Suffice it to say that I've spent his last $1.98 for sheer, sheer stockings that won't run. They didn't run. Instead they exploded silently into a huge mushroom-shaped hole at the knee the first time I put them on.

I plead guilty to having tried everything from stockings guaranteed not to run down (I always snag them in the ankle) to those guaranteed not to run up (I always snag them near the top). And when I'm seen in public with a run, I no longer pretend that it just appeared. It's *been* there, maybe not quite so wide, but it's been there for the last five times I've worn stockings.

As for shoes with heels that have doubled the business of flooring manufacturers, bunion removers, crutch makers and tranquilizer distributors (can *you* stay calm when your Ladies' Aid Society leaves the expensive new linoleum looking as if it had died with small-pox?), well . . . WELL?

Do women's fashions make sense? Ask any husband—and then duck.

Better yet, keep him ignorant of some of the vagaries of the fashion world by refusing to adopt nonsensical unbecoming ex-tremes. After all, you're not interested in competing for a new man, you're trying to keep your old one safe from apoplexy.

Remember *that* when you're contemplating other extravagances too. Keeping up with the Joneses is highly recommended—for keep-ing your marriage down in the dumps.

4

Casting Stones

SPARED TROUBLES with in-laws and drinking and money, we did have other problems to grow by.

Once, in a letter, I asked my fiancé if he had a temper. "Yes," he wrote back, "I have a terrible temper. I hope you'll never have to see it."

That hope wasn't to be realized. I can remember one day when I thought he was going to shake a recalcitrant washing machine to pieces to cure it of the perversity of inanimate objects.

At first I was upset by his infrequent displays of temper. But temper was contagious, and before long I found that I, who had thought myself born without a temper, agreed with him that inanimate objects were not inanimate at all. They were diabolical demons in disguise.

That wasn't a particularly happy revelation, but it did let me understand my husband. Helpless under the occasional tyranny of my own temper, I sympathized with him when he was the unwilling victim of his. No longer could I secretly condemn him for his outbursts.

We soon learned, to my sorrow, that my faults were contagious

too. One of my college roommates, pleased that Allen and I were
to be married, wrote, "I always liked Allen. He never had anything
bad to say about anyone, did he?"

No, he didn't. Not until he had lived with me for a while. Then
he came down with the dread disease I carried—that of being
critical of other people. Now, when I shrink at his criticism of someone I realize it's my fault. He learned criticism from me.

If we'd known how contagious our faults were, we might have
been more careful not to expose each other. But valuable understanding came from seeing our own faults mirrored back. It helped
me realize that correcting myself must come first. I needed to get all
the beams out of my own eyes before I could presume to remove
any motes from his.

Since neither of us was perfect it was inevitable that we would
have differences of opinion. We didn't usually *say* anything—grace,
even unsought, had been given us to know that words left unsaid
were easier undone. I know that's not what the modern psychia-
trists advise, but it has worked for us. I think silence can preserve
the sanctity of marriage far better than "hashing it out."

Our actions sometimes spoke volumes, though. Righteous indignation, to use a polite term for it, can be vented in more constructive ways than in verbal battles, anyhow.

I remember one night, years ago, when we weren't "prayer and
church people" like we are now. All the kids—there were four of
them by that time—were finally tucked in bed for the night. I was
up to my elbows in dirty dishes and supposed *he* was reading the
paper or doing something equally innocuous in the living room—
cutting his toenails, maybe.

Then he walked into the kitchen all necktied up with the announcement that he thought he'd take in a late movie at the
theater—if it was all right with me.

I managed a teeth-gritting smile and refrained from expressing
my real thoughts on the subject while I accepted his peck on the
cheek and maintained my outward equilibrium until the car slid
out of the driveway. Then, righteous indignation took over. (It
still helps to keep using a relatively calm word for it.)

IMAGINE! Twice in less than a week he had left me for the late movie. And I didn't know where the money was coming from for the bills that were piled on top of the refrigerator—the only place the kids hadn't learned to climb to yet. I'd have liked to have gone to the movies—or anywhere—occasionally myself, but I'd nothing to wear and the sitter wanted fifty cents an hour. Besides that, my shoes were so out of style and shape I had to tuck my feet under wherever I went.

No wonder I was getting so fat. Four babies in five years and I thought I was expecting again and the little baby only six months old! I hadn't seen a living soul except my husband, the children, and the garbage man for months, it seemed like. Where would I have got the incentive to do anything *but* stuff myself constantly when I had no social life? Not even a television to let me see other adults once in a while. It wasn't so bad in summer, but mid-January with all the kids having colds was pretty gruesome. Honestly, sometimes I wondered if it was worth it.

But wait a minute. I knew I'd better keep on doing the dishes while I was feeling sorry for myself. One of the lesser known facts of life at our house was that if I didn't wash the supper dishes the kids were sure to want pancakes for breakfast instead of cereal in bowls. The bowls were the only clean things in the cupboard.

But I could cry loud as anything while I was washing the dishes. It *was* more satisfactory before we got those unbreakable plastic ones.

When the dishes were finished, several alternatives beckoned. I could go to bed crying as long as I could make the tears last, thinking of all the mean or inconsiderate things he had done lately. But that would have been a waste of time and there was always *so* much work to be done. Besides, the movie would probably be so long he wouldn't even notice I'd been crying when he got home, and what good would that do?

I could decide to read a book and enjoy it, but I certainly didn't want to *enjoy* anything. I had to be a martyr. And that meant WORK.

The adrenalin that rushes through your system when you are all huffed up about something has magic output qualities—have you never noticed? So I made up my mind I might just as well use it on something that needed doing. I'd get through in half the usual time without even trying. A disagreeable task would be the best to choose because with all my anger turned in *his* direction I'd be wonderfully efficient and wouldn't mind the job nearly as much.

I couldn't tackle the ironing or the mending or anything else that was supposed to be my job anyway. I had to choose something that should have been his responsibility, preferably something I'd been hinting at for some time. I wanted to make him feel guilty, you seé, without saying a word about it.

How about scrubbing the kitchen walls? Perfect!

That particular job had several things about it which made it ideal for my purpose. It involved climbing on a step stool or that rickety ladder, standing precariously on counter tops, reaching as far as I could, and moving the refrigerator, stove, and automatic washer away from the walls. All of these maneuvers I knew I could execute with perfect safety but he'd be sure to fuss about them.

I didn't expect him to notice that I had washed the walls, but he could hardly avoid seeing the appliances I'd leave out for him to push back into place, the presence of the ladder, the bucket of dirty water, the footprints on the counters, and the pile of junk I had retrieved from under the refrigerator. While I was about it, I polished the bottoms of the copper pans hanging on the wall. That didn't take long but made such a difference in the looks of the room that even *he* might notice.

The timing in the scrubbing was vitally important and I paid close attention to it. I had to be sure there was enough debris left scattered that he'd know I'd been slaving away, but I had to be equally certain I was finished with the actual *work* by the time he came in. There'd be no sense in my killing myself working when he was right there to ignore the fact. I would just get mad—I mean righteously indignant—all over again, and then I might have to scrub the *living room* walls as well.

Nor could I answer the telephone if it rang when it was time for him to come home either. It would just be a wrong number, but he'd be sure to catch me at it and think I'd spent the whole evening gabbing.

I didn't plan to wash my face or brush my hair before he came in. I wanted to look rosy-cheeked, slightly smudged, attractively rumpled and steamy from honest exertion. It would have taken more than Academy Award talent to simulate the whole business. I had to *do* the work!

Of course my tears subsided long before he got home and I'd used up so much adrenalin scrubbing that I wasn't even interested in a fight. The five-cent coke he brought me provided such a welcome break that he thought I was glad to see *him!*

First thing I knew I was sympathizing with him about the movie's not being too good. And he was so interested in getting to the sports page that he didn't realize I'd been put out at all. And it *was* nice to have that dirty kitchen clean after all those weeks of wishing about it.

There I was, a tired but contented wife, honestly thankful for a husband who didn't drink or run around with other women.

He still doesn't—and he gave up smoking long ago—and he doesn't go to the movies without me any more either. But not because I nagged at him about it. Allen never has been the kind of man you could nag and get away with it. And I'm glad—I'd have been a bad one.

My husband grew, partly because I let him. And he gave me a chance to grow too. I certainly needed it.

Being righteously indignant instead of trying to be sympathetically understanding that Allen was not immune to the pressures of life wasn't lovely, I know. But if my ferocious action kept me from vituperative words I'd have regretted, and thus protected what *was* right and happy in our relationship, it had its uses.

I think often about the Ogden Nash verse that contains so much truth and wisdom:

> To keep your marriage brimming
> With love in the loving cup,
> Whenever you're wrong, admit it
> Whenever you're right, shut up.

I thank my God for every time I've been able to exercise the last line of, it especially. There's little practical "worldly" advice that's worth more.

Allen and I decided, long ago, that when each of us has attained perfection in *all* things—*including humility*—we'll be in a position to correct each other. And not before then. Present indications are that we'll have a long wait.

I won't go into all our other faults and how they've provided avenues for understanding and growth, but there are plenty of them. We believe that faults are to a marriage what garbage is to a garden: rotted down, they make perfect composting material to make a marriage richer and more productive of good things.

5

Kids' Capers

CHILDREN GIVE you opportunities to grow in patience and under-standing—if you cultivate a sense of humor and if you can stand the pace. When our "big four" were small, we were still young enough and tough enough to survive, some times triumphantly.

I have a dim recollection of a conversation with an across-the-street neighbor who had four children of her own. They were a little older than mine.

"Your children never bother you, do they, Irene?" She asked it with a trace of envy in her voice.

"Bother me? What do you mean?" I didn't understand her question at all. Why should the children bother me? I mean, after all, I *was* their mother, and they *were* my children. I didn't have anything to do except to stay at home and take care of them. They were cute; they did fight sometimes, but I could paddle them and put them to bed whenever the occasion called for it. There was no reason to be *bothered* by them that I could think of.

She laughed and nodded with her longer years of experience. "That's fine. You'll find out what I mean sometime. It's good you get along so well with them now."

She was right. I did find out. There came a time when I had things I wanted to do other than stay at home all the time and take care of my children. Then's when frustration sets in, when you have things to do that conflict with what the children require of you. It happens after you get outside activities, or they do, or you're trying to prepare a company meal, or get the house ready to receive guests. Then the delays children force upon you are not so delightful to cope with. It's the fractioning of our lives that fractures us so.

Inklings of future discord come in many ways. They're almost invariably nice to recall but a little hectic to live through at the time. We're too close to what goes on, I guess. Take the day of the circus.

Planning for Monday's playground circus had apparently been going on for weeks, but it was late Sunday afternoon when I first got wind of it. I don't know why I never heard of such things until the very last minute. Maybe it was just as well.

My four cherubs had just marched into the kitchen where I was putting the finishing touches on the casserole for the church supper.

"Mama, we're going to have a circus tomorrow, and I get to be a—" I couldn't quite make out the rest of it, until I broke up the chorus and heard one part at a time.

I had one lion, one lion-tamer, one clown, one magician and a sinking feeling in the middle of my head, heart, and stomach. The stores were closed, we were all due at the church at six o'clock, and it would be bedtime for the kids when we got home.

"Well, I'm sorry, but you should have told me sooner," I said, thankful that they hadn't mentioned it in time for me to do anything. "We can't get ready at this late notice, can we? They'll have to have the circus without you. You can just watch the others."

There. That was that. I had been firm. I was proud of myself for not having gone all to pieces and tried to do what was clearly impossible. After all, even Barnum and Bailey require a *little* advance notice.

"Now run along and get ready for church," I said as I wrung

out the dishrag and hung it on the edge of the sink. I thought I had handled the situation rather well—until I saw their faces.

Quiet tears were welling up in Susan's eyes. They didn't look as if they'd stay quiet long. Her mouth was a perfect half-circle, turned down. It was beginning to wiggle a little around the edges.

"But, Mama, I could wear James's leopard pajamas, couldn't I? They'd make me look *almost* like a lion."

I've always been a sucker for logic. Those pajamas, bought three Hallowe'ens ago, *could* have one final fling before being consigned to the ragbag for good.

"Maybe, Susan, maybe. Quit crying and see if you can find them. I know they'll need mending first."

I was hoping there were actually enough shreds of them left *for* mending.

James stopped rubbing his eyes with the back of his fist.

"Oh, boy! Then I can be a leopard-tamer instead of a lion-tamer, can't I, Mom? I'll just need a reg'lar chair and I'll make me a whip out of something. Can I—please, Mom?"

The "please, Mom" did it. I'm always impressed when the kids are polite without my having to remind them.

"Well, I guess so. Only you'll have to be careful with a whip—" He didn't hear all of it, because he had zoomed out of the door into the yard. Too late I found out that the whip he had in mind was a long waving branch from our neighbor's favorite flowering shrub!

Alice was next in line. She wasn't about to cry. She knew that I'd been licked.

"Being a clown is easy," she said. "I can just put on some of Daddy's baggy old clothes and look stupid. And can I have one of your silly hats?"

She took my moan to mean "Yes," and I decided I might just as well be gracious in defeat.

"Now, Tom, that leaves you, I guess. What did you have in mind?"

When will I learn not to ask what he has in mind? It might be easier to talk him out of if I didn't let him say it out loud.

Tom scrambled from the floor where he had flopped in a dejected heap at the first disappointment.

"Well, I'm going to be a magician, and I thought I could saw Alice in two, and jerk a tablecloth out from under your dishes, and I'd learn some Indian rope tricks, or something like that." He finished a little lamely, as if it had occurred to him that some of those things might not be agreeable to me.

I thought of suggesting that he build the Taj Mahal overnight. It would be just as possible as what he had in mind, and a lot prettier, but I didn't say so. My "Honestly, Tom" probably conveyed my feelings adequately.

"Well, maybe I'll think of something that will work. Anyway, I'm the only magician they're going to have so I've *got* to do *something.*"

On the way to church he and Alice decided that he could pull things out of a black hat. That would make a good act for his part of the sideshow and Alice could be his hidden assistant until time for her clown performance. They extracted a promise from me that they could stay up later than usual that night to work on their props.

The carport buzzed with activity when we got home. A big old box Tom had begged from the washer repairman on his last visit was just right for the magician's table. Turned on its side it was exactly the right height, and Alice could crawl in the open end to hide herself from view.

The kids rounded up scissors, an old sheet, and some black construction paper, and proceeded to convert the washing machine carton into prop number one. They cut a hole in the sheet to match the hole in the box where the hidden assistant would hand objects into the apparently empty hat. The black paper became stars, moons, suns, Saturns, lightning flashes and other mysterious signs of the zodiac for decoration.

Tom wanted to paint decorations on the sheet instead, but I'd had experience with Tom and paint before and learned that almost anything else—including the bubonic plague—was preferable.

The scissors were also used to harvest a pile of grass to bed down a bulging-eyed frog that had, all unsuspecting, wandered into the carport. The kids decided not to dismember him on the spot (every day some small miracle occurred for which I was duly thankful) but to keep him alive overnight so that he could magically appear from the hat.

It was morning before I tackled the hat construction job. All the black paper had been used for zodiac decorations, but, ever resourceful (with four kids I could never *expect* to use anything for the purpose for which I bought it), I unstuck Grandpa and scenic views of the Smoky Mountains from my largest photograph album. With the album pages and a few paper clips and staples I managed to create the stovepipe part of the hat.

Fashioning the brim was relatively easy. "Relatively easy"— when it's past time to go, the kids are having a grand difference of opinion about whose turn it is to sit in the front seat, the phone is ringing its head off, and the egg man is waiting at the door to be paid—may be harder than you think.

Attaching the top of the hat so that it would seem solid and still allow the passage of livestock wasn't so simple. It wouldn't have been quite so impossible if we hadn't been out of glue. Someone had emptied the glue the week before in order to use the little rubber-tipped bottle to feed a didie-doll.

We were out of tape, too. All the adhesive tape, as well as the cellophane variety, had been used up by James a few days before when he had a microscopic scratch on his finger. He had supposed mummy-style wrapping was in order and had proceeded accordingly. When I found him, his finger was nearly as fat as an oversized roll of bologna and the skin beneath the windings *had* almost mummified.

In desperation I attached the top of the hat with straight pins and hoped they'd hold until we got to the playground.

Mournful wails came from the direction of the carport where the kids had just discovered that their frog had disappeared from the box during the night. There wasn't time to catch another, so we improvised a rabbit from a tennis ball wrapped in a white handkerchief.

We arrived at the park just in time for the big show to begin. I caught up on my breathing while Tom and Alice hurriedly set up their magic show.

The audience flocked around the magician's table during the

intermission. I should call it "endshow" instead of sideshow because the first thing anyone saw was the retreating, baggy, seat-of-the-pants of the clown crawling into the sheet-covered box. The sheet-covered box looked like just that, there having been neither time nor stickum to apply the fascinating black decorations so laboriously cut out the night before.

The next thing visible to those waiting patiently for something magic to happen was Tom's careful adjusting of the sheet's hole to match the hole in the box. That done, he mouthed at me, where I was standing inconspicuously, in the back row of spectators, "I can't find the hat, Mama!"

When I pretended not to see him—what else could I do?—he shrugged, lowered his shoulders and eyebrows to normal, cleared his throat importantly, and announced, "I am a magician. I will now draw a baby rabbit out of this hat—I mean box."

Reaching his hand in the hole, he waited, and waited, and waited. Finally, withdrawing his still empty hand, he put his mouth to the hole and said, in a voice sufficiently peevish for all to hear, "Alice, give me the rabbit!"

The sheet hanging loose over the open end of the box bulged a little, and then out came Alice's head, her eyes all but overflowing.

"The rabbit's not in here, Tom. Nothing's in here but me."

Tom's "Excuse me just a second, folks," was nothing if not professional. All eyes turned in my direction as he elbowed his way through the thinning crowd.

"Mama, she lost the rabbit. What should I do now?" Tom looked ready to agree to anything.

I wanted to disown him, or sink into the ground, or grab him and run, but it was too late for any of those. Remembering the white gloves in my purse, I rummaged quickly, extracted them, and fashioned a white lump with two ear-like projections.

Tom carried the contraption admiringly before him to the box, where he lifted the sheet on the open end and stooped for a short conference with his sister, handing the glove-rabbit to her.

Then, pulling himself to his full height, smiling and looking very handsome in his white shirt and blue tie, he announced confidently,

"*Now*, I will *now* pull a rabbit from this hat—I mean box."

At that signal a small hand pushed up through the hole, bearing a beginning-to-come-undone pair of white gloves in it. I suppose Alice just *had* to find out how we'd made the rabbit. Tom took them in his right hand, shoved her hand back in the box with his left, and held the pair of gloves triumphantly aloft.

One glove fell to the ground before the applause ended, and Alice, curious about all the clapping, stuck her head out to see what was going on.

With a disgusted look at her, Tom announced, "Last night we caught a frog, and I was going to draw him out of the box, too, but he got away. So that's all, folks!"

A few chuckles and a sprinkling of disappointed "aw's" greeted this news, and the spectators gradually moved on to the leopard-taming act. Not me, though. I didn't have the nerve.

I slunk back to the car with a firm resolve. I had grown in wisdom that day. The next time someone said, "Mama, we're going to have a circus and I get to be in it," I would pull a disappearing act of my own.

6

Book L'arnin'

A COMPLAINT familiar to marriage counselors is "We just don't have anything in common any more." That always strikes a chord of incredulity in me, especially when it comes from husbands and wives who've raised a family. Why, they've probably eaten the same food and occupied the same physical and emotional environment for so long that they've actually begun to *look* alike. They're bound to have more in common than when they were married.

We didn't have much in common at the beginning either—except that we were both in love. And that proved to be more than enough to have in common until our lives together provided the rest.

We shared in all that was trivial, all that was vital. Everything— babies, bills, vitamins, tricycles, diapers, umbrellas, toothpaste, dis- appointments, books—everything was "in common." The list is endless, a weaving together of the whole warp and woof of our lives.

But ignorance furnished the "in common" element that was to prove the best marriage cement of all. Ignorance? Helpful in a marriage? Some would suppose knowledge to be of more benefit. But let me tell you.

Somewhere along the line we discovered that we had in common an abysmal ignorance of everything that really mattered. He had joined the church, once, and continued to attend occasionally. And sometimes he read the Bible a little. But I didn't belong to a church and actually had some trouble remembering that Matthew, Mark, Luke and John were in the New Testament.

I can't pinpoint when our lives began to orient themselves toward God. It was when He turned us around, I suppose. I know we weren't always obviously headed in the right direction. We began to study the Bible, to read the lives of the saints and classic devotional literature. I joined the church and we started to teach Sunday School together.

Together we discovered St. Paul, and Augustine, Francis of Assisi, Brother Lawrence, and John Woolman, Martin Luther, Thomas Kelly and William Barclay—and a host of others. Could any marriage fail to be strengthened by such company? Here was the most exciting adventure imaginable! We found our ignorance-in-common the best blessing of all. It helped in lots of ways.

"I've simply *got* to have a new pair of shoes!" My tone must have been more than a little complaining as I contemplated the hole in the sole of my Sunday-best pumps and rubbed my fingers over the shiny spots in the worn suede.

"Really?" My husband had an amused twinkle in his eye. "I can see it's time for you to read about St. Francis again."

His comment wouldn't have made sense to everybody, but it did to me. Studying St. Francis together a few years before had made economy, even frugality, easy for us. St. Francis's love for "Lady Poverty" and his thankfulness for the riches of the gifts of God had made a not-to-be-forgotten impact on our lives.

My husband was right, I mused, as I trimmed a cornflake boxtop to line my shoe. It was past time for me to refresh my memory, and my soul, with St. Francis, for I had begun to fret over the restrictions of a sometimes snug budget instead of thanking God that we had enough to eat and to wear and a roof over our heads.

As I blew a thin layer of dust from the top of our copy of *The Little Flowers of St. Francis* I thought about how much that little volume and other devotional classics had meant to us.

One I frequently recommend to people who complain of too much to do (and reread for myself when I am so calendered-up with unessential activities and responsibilities that I find myself neglecting my more important obligations) is Thomas Kelly's *Testament of Devotion*.

I'll never forget the first time I read it, nor the effect of the last chapter, "The Simplification of Life." I found myself nodding in agreement with all this modern Quaker had to say about how the confusion of the outside world is not responsible for our own confusions and frustrations. He says that the problem lies within us. If we were properly attentive to our "inner light" and dedicated ourselves to following it, our frantic activity would cease. Our lives would become purposeful and fruitful.

It was late at night when I finished reading the book. I went up to bed with a peculiar peace and resolution in my heart. The next day I wrote a letter resigning as chairman of a committee, one of which I should not have been even a member because its purpose did not fit in with what I thought God intended for my life.

Don't make the mistake of thinking that the simplification of life means only saying "no" to responsibilities the world wants to thrust upon you. It also means saying "yes"—a wholehearted, unreserved, uncomplaining "yes"—to jobs you believe God wants you to undertake. And, instead of finding your life fragmented by them, you'll feel it growing into an ever more significant whole, a "testament of devotion" itself.

Another book, exceedingly helpful and consoling when you are aware of problems with your children in their sometimes restless search for truth, is *The Confessions of St. Augustine*. Augustine was a wild youth if ever there was one. He tells of stealing, not because he wanted something he couldn't afford, but simply for the love of doing evil. He was ashamed not to be the worst one in his crowd.

When Augustine was only a teenager he fathered an illegitimate child, and during years of living a worldly life he embraced one heretical religion after another. His mother's despair led her to consult the bishop, who assured her that as yet Augustine was "unteachable" but that there was no chance that the child of her tears and prayers would fail to discover the truth of God.

And the bishop was right. Augustine's own account of his conversion ranks with the most famous literature of all time.

One special little quotation from *The Confessions* hangs around the neck of our cookie jar, there to admonish us if we become smug about not drinking and forget that other overindulgences are also bad. "Drunkenness is far from me," Augustine wrote, "but overeating has sometimes crept upon Thy servant."

A devotional classic that seemed familiar to me the first time I read it was Thomas à Kempis' *Of the Imitation of Christ*. That's because it weaves in so many passages from the Bible. *The Imitation* has appeared in thousands of editions and has sold more copies than any book except the Bible.

One of my favorite passages from this book is: "If only your heart were right, then every created thing would be to you a mirror of life and a book of holy teaching." I prop that in the forefront of my mind when I might be tempted to be cynical or downcast about life. It helps me remember that getting my heart right is my task—only then can I have faith in God's purpose in all things.

That quotation fits well alongside our Romans 8:28, "We know that in everything God works for good with those who love him, who are called according to his purpose." Examining any adversity in the light of these two passages helps me see that God has meaning for everything in my life.

If Allen and I had to limit ourselves to one devotional book (in addition to the Bible) we'd be bound to consider a tiny one entitled *The Practice of the Presence of God* by Brother Lawrence. Brother Lawrence was a humble man, so full of love for God that he could pray as well in the clanging surroundings of the busy scullery where he worked as a cook's helper as on his knees at the holy sacrament.

Somehow, reading his brief pages at the end of a day, however hectic it's been, can calm and soothe you for the next one. "Practicing the presence" makes it possible for you to lay aside cares and troubles that seem beyond your patience or bearing, and embrace the peace that passes understanding.

"Take and read, take and read," in the singsong voice of a child, led Augustine to pick up a book and draw closer to his Lord. Now,

centuries later, we too draw closer to the same Lord when we read
scripture and other devotional literature. Reading of devotional
classics provides a blessed rendezvous where the grace of God can
meet the seeking heart of man.

And if, as you take and read, your soul mate shares the hearthside
with you and you share your reading and insights with him, and he
with you, you build a bond of understanding on the deepest, highest
levels, for He is in the midst of you, just as He promised: "For
where two or three are gathered together in my name, there am I in
the midst of them" (Matthew 18:20, KJV). And His being in the
midst of you will surely change your lives. It did ours, rather drama-
tically, years after we considered ourselves already "saved," but I'll
keep that for the last chapter.

In the meantime, we were no longer concerned about seeking a
happy marriage for ourselves. That had already been given us,
above all we could ask or think. A good marriage must be one of the
"things" He promises when He says, "Seek ye first the kingdom of
God, and his righteousness; and all these *things* shall be added unto
you." Seek to grow toward Him, by His grace. That's all the
formula you need for a growing marriage.

Eph.
3:20

Matt.
6:33

7

Plans of Mice and Men

A BAD CASE of bronchitis had sent me to the doctor. It had been hanging on, keeping me awake at night with paroxysms of coughing and breathing difficulties.

During his examination the doctor looked at the red splotches on my face and chest. I had noticed them that morning, but had given them no particular thought, assuming that the "ailing-est" winter of my life was bound to be reflected in my complexion sooner or later.

"That looks like rubella to me," the doctor said, "Been around any of it lately?"

"Rubella?" The word sounded vaguely familiar, but I couldn't think just what it meant.

"German measles. Three-day measles," he explained as he tucked his stethoscope back into his pocket.

"Oh, yes! The kids had three-day measles just a couple of weeks ago. But I thought I had it when I was a little girl."

"Maybe you did, and maybe you didn't. Anyway, you have it now, or I miss my guess. Come on in the office when you're dressed and we'll see what we can do for the bronchitis. There's nothing to be done about the rubella. You'll just get over that."

He left the small white examining room, closing behind him the sliding door into his walnut-panelled office.

I smiled over the ridiculousness of having a childhood disease, at *my* age, until the crisply starched nurse asked me a question: "You're not pregnant, are you?" She looked at me seriously.

"Why, no. I'm sure I'm not," I answered confidently as I finished dressing. Thinking about her question for a minute I had to admit to myself that I had been aware of a few things that might mean I was pregnant.

But I couldn't be.

Four children were enough. Our decision not to have any more babies had been made several years ago, after a frightening miscarriage. We had realized then that the children with which we were already blessed needed me far more than they needed another brother or sister. And we hadn't changed our minds.

But suppose I was pregnant? What then? I had been reading in the newspapers that German measles during the early months of pregnancy could result in a deformed child.

By the next morning my mirror confirmed the doctor's opinion about the rubella. I was a sight!

After all the spots had disappeared I had the arthritic swelling in my fingers the doctor had warned me to expect. "Now don't worry," he'd said. "This stiffness and swelling won't mean that you're having another spell of rheumatoid arthritis. It'll go away in just a day or two. Quite common after German measles. I just wanted you to be prepared for it."

For several weeks I kept telling myself that I could not be pregnant. I was probably just anemic or something. A winter of sore throat, arthritis, bronchitis, and measles, together with the responsibilities of a full-time away-from-home job, a lively family of four grade-schoolers and no household help was surely enough to make anyone a little run-down.

I was glad we had decided to let me take the next year off, to be just a housewife for a change. Our twelve wonderful years of marriage had included four babies, one miscarriage, and eight years of library work for me. We all felt I was entitled to a breather, and I had not signed a contract for the next academic year.

I was looking forward to time to be a better mother, to listen to the kids for a change, to be a real wife and show more interest in my husband's recital of what went on in his office without having to burden him with my working woes. And I was going to give myself time at the typewriter to see if I could write. If I could prove myself a success at that in a year's time, I wouldn't have to go back to work again.

But instead of going away, symptoms of pregnancy stayed with me. Soon, in addition to the first symptoms, I had others I couldn't ignore: a downright unfashionable circumference, an elephantine appetite for any edible in sight, and an unconquerable drowsiness, no matter how much sleep I got. I was ready to see our obstetrician.

It didn't take him long to confirm my suspicions. Later I sat down in his office for what turned out to be a prolonged and significant conference. I asked lots of questions. The doctor didn't minimize the hazards of German measles, but he didn't suggest an abortion either.

At any rate my husband and I had already made up our minds. God had blessed us with four perfectly beautiful, normal children. If it was our turn to be entrusted with one who needed special care, we would welcome the opportunity.

In our experience we had found that where God gives a problem He is generous in bestowing the faith and courage to meet it, transforming it into a blessing—a special gift from God.

There was another decision to be made, too. The sharp pain I had felt in my abdomen during one of the bronchitis coughing spells had been the beginning of hernia. I had noticed how the place swelled and ached painfully whenever I had to be on my feet for long stretches at a time.

"You can have that fixed next week," the obstetrician told me, "or wait until the baby is a few months old and have it fixed next year."

I couldn't see leaving a new baby in order to have an operation and then not be able to pick it up or to take care of it during weeks of careful convalescence. "Couldn't I wait just a month until my scheduled vacation from work?" I asked.

" 'Fraid not. It's now or next year. In another month you'll be too full of baby for an incision to heal easily. And of course there's the chance that you might have to have an emergency operation for the hernia at some less advisable time during your pregnancy. If I were you . . ."

He had me persuaded. I imagine I gulped, thinking of all the things I had planned to finish up at work during the next month, but I said, "Well, next week, then."

"Okay, who do you want to do the operation?"

Why did my husband have to be out of town today, of all days? I knew by sight only one of the surgeons the obstetrician named, but I had heard friends speak favorably of him and his ability. A few minutes later we had been introduced and he was on the telephone making the necessary operating-room reservation.

When he turned from the phone to say, "You'll want a private room, I suppose," with hardly a question in his voice, I had to suppress a laugh. I certainly didn't *feel* prosperous, and couldn't imagine how the events of the morning could have made me look that way.

"No, let me have a bed in a ward, please. That's what the insurance pays for." Under my breath I added, "I hope." We hadn't used our hospitalization for such a long time I didn't know *what* it provided.

I went to work the next day, for the last time, and left my office in remarkably good order, considering. My staff was too dumbfounded to say much, except to wish me luck.

The operation the next week went along without a hitch, and my convalescence was so uneventful I was released from the hospital a day ahead of schedule. I took seriously the doctor's "absolutely no exertion for a month" and arranged for the two months' full-time household help he said I should have.

When the maid quit after a week, tired of washing windows and afraid I was going to ask her to tackle the woodwork on Monday, we considered trying to find other help, but decided to use the summer to let the children grow up instead.

From my couch I could direct them in whatever chores had to be done. Before I was completely back on my feet again I had the cutest crew of bed makers, clothes folders, table setters, rug shakers, wastebasket emptiers and floor sweepers in town. They brought me what I needed at the range so I could do the cooking from a perch on a high stool. Their bulging allowance jars were evidence of the money they earned that would otherwise have been paid to someone else. And there was lots of time left for play.

8

Getting "It" Done

As I recovered from my operation I resumed more than my former share of the household chores. But not for long.

"I don't see why there has to be such a thing as teeth. They don't do you any good." Eight-year-old James glowered at me as he grumped his way to the bathroom and jerked his toothbrush out of the rack. I'd have had to laugh if I hadn't been so exasperated. I'd already reminded him three times that morning to brush his teeth and then had caught him about to scoot out the door for school without doing it.

And it wasn't just James. The other children had become just as lax about their responsibilities. It seemed to me they were being less helpful every day, and were finding more things to complain about.

It hadn't been that way when I'd come home from the hospital. The kids had been wonderfully helpful then. I'd not had to nag at all, and reminding was seldom necessary. I'd never seen the kids happier.

Now I was making the beds, emptying wastebaskets, and picking up toys and clothes after all of them. Such simple requests as, "Will you come and set the table for me, please, Alice?" met with a frown and a complaining, "I don't see why you don't make Susan do it. She never has to do anything!" And so, before long, to avoid unpleasantness, I quit asking for help and seemed to be doing everything myself.

Not that I minded. Keeping house after several years of working away from home was fun to me. Our new home was so conveniently arranged and so well equipped with labor-saving devices I didn't really need any help. I enjoyed every housewifely chore, almost as if it had been play.

But that wasn't the point. There was another side of it. Instead of being increasingly carefree and happy because they no longer had chores to do, the children were gradually becoming unbearable little gripers, never satisfied with anything. They criticized their clothing, their food, their teachers, their friends, one another, and even themselves.

At breakfast one morning all of the children were horribly cross. During a lull in the crossfire of argument and criticism Susan said wistfully, "Wouldn't it be wonderful if, before the baby is born, we would all learn to be nice, so the baby would never hear any ugly talk?" Her words were strangely prophetic but I didn't know it then. I couldn't have guessed that although we didn't learn to be nice, our baby-to-be would live most of her first year happily insulated from any unpleasant sounds around her.

"What makes me so stupid?" was the tearful lament of the oldest the day he had to stay in with a sore throat, knowing it had come from his sneaking out without a coat or cap on a really blustery day that week. "I oughtta be dead!"

What had happened? Why had the good discipline and high spirits of the summer disintegrated overnight? My husband and I kept making excuses to each other. "Well, they're so busy with their school work," or, "It's because some of their friends aren't expected to help around the house." But I think we both suspected that something more basic was wrong.

With a new baby on the way I had to get the other children straightened out at once.

Puffing from the exertion of bending over to pick up the game the kids had left strewn in the middle of the family room floor, I found myself thinking, "Well, at least I'm getting it done," and then is when the real trouble dawned on me. The "it" of straightening the house was not the "it" that needed doing at all!

Since resigning from my nine-to-five job I had been thinking of myself as a housewife—a being whose primary job was keeping house. Like the little red hen, I occasionally asked for volunteers, but finding no one eager to help me, had said, "Very well, then, I'll do it myself."

Suddenly I realized that my primary job was not keeping house. Anyone could do that. My first responsibility was to rear my children, trying to instill in them some of the attitudes and habits that would mold character, making their lives useful and happy ones. Doing the housework myself was easy, but it meant that I was utterly abandoning the far more important job of training my children.

I needed to change course—but fast. Something had to be done. Could there be any connection between the kids' general dissatisfaction and the fact that I was no longer requiring anything of them?

Why not? It works that way for adults. When we feel not needed, we're miserable. When much is required of us, we rise to the challenge. When we seem to be almost indispensable we're in our glory. Couldn't it be that way with children too? It was worth a try.

How lucky that I would be going to the hospital soon. There could be no better time to let the children get back into their habits of helpfulness around the house than right now. I could hardly wait for three o'clock when they were due to come home from school.

I'd not wait until the new baby arrived. I'd begin today, assigning each child to a set of regular jobs again, letting each be responsible for his own chores in a way that left no room nor necessity for nagging. And I'd never stop again. Because the training would be for the sake of the children, not for the sake of the housewife.

I began to bet that the homework that came after supper wouldn't need almost physical prodding from me to get done, either. Kids are a lot like grownups—they can measure up to your expectations—if you expect enough. I hoped I would measure up too and get "it" done, now that I realize what "it" really was.

How could I be so confident? The kids themselves had told me the answer that summer, when they didn't know I was listening. I guess at the time I didn't get the full significance of it.

Tom and Alice were collaborating on the sweeping of the carport. When I looked out the window Alice had stopped for a minute to brush the hair back out of her face. "You know, Tom," she said, "I don't care if we *don't* have as much fun as other kids. At least we're being brought up right!"

Tom quit his whistling just long enough to nod at her and say proudly, "Me too!"

9

Our "Expecting" Family

"MAMA, I DON'T see why the doctor has to *deliver* our baby. Because you'll have to be right there in the same room when he's born." Seven-year-old Susan, our "old baby," was shaking her head, clearly perplexed by some of the grownup talk she'd been hearing.

I hugged her up to me, and, when I could trust myself not to laugh, explained. "Susan, 'deliver' is like a lot of other words you know. It doesn't always mean the same thing. When we say that a doctor 'delivers' a baby we just mean that he helps it to be born."

"Oh, I see! But you'll still bring it home yourself, when you come from the hospital." At my confirmation she nodded her head up and down, understanding.

I was learning so much about my family and the ways of the child mind during the months before our "new baby" came out. I know that's a rather inelegant way to put it, and I had corrected eight-year-old James on numerous occasions when he persisted in saying, "When the baby comes out . . . ."

"Say, 'When the baby is born,' James; it sounds better," I admonished him. The other expression made me wince. It sounded too clinical to my over-sensitive adult ears.

50

"Okay, Mom." He was always very willing to comply and would rephrase his question, but five minutes later he'd have something else to ask and would begin again, "Mama, after the baby comes out" until I finally gave up.

I didn't understand until after I went to PTA one night. On each third grader's desk was a picture the child had drawn that day. All were captioned: "If I go to the moon I will carry these things in my pocket." Many of the drawings had identical objects in them, all logical—flashlights, knives, hammers and toothbrushes.

But James' drawing had two unique objects as well—a baby bottle and a pacifier. The pictures were readily identifiable even if the spelling was a little bit individualistic. James was going to be ready for that baby no matter where he was!

That's when I realized why the children kept saying, "When the baby comes out." To them, the baby was not something we were going to have later, after it was born. We had it now. The baby was somebody real, even though it was still cradled in my body. Hadn't they felt it kick and roll and have hiccups? How could they think of it in terms of something yet to be when they knew its acrobatics could already qualify it for top billing with Barnum and Bailey?

My husband and I learned something from their insight. However we might express ourselves in words, we too were thinking in terms of "when the baby comes out. . . ." That means we were enjoying and loving him, acknowledging him as a part of our family without waiting for his actual birthday. Chinese fashion, I think we'll regard him as already nearly a year old on the date the doctor writes on the birth certificate.

His coming was certainly well advertised. Children tickled to death about something can't keep secrets, and we hadn't expected them to try. Sharing the good news about the baby was an important part of their enjoyment.

There had been a few times when I wished they'd been a little more decorous about it than Alice, then nine years old, was one Sunday morning. We'd just been introduced to some dignified-looking visitors on the church steps. One commented, "Two boys and two girls, what a nice family."

Alice couldn't resist telling, in tones proud enough for the whole congregation to hear, "Yes! But Mama's gonna have a baby! And then we'll be uneven, unless she has *twins!*" By the time she had reached the end of her gleeful announcement she was almost squealing.

My midsection must have blushed at the Sunday stares, but the steps refused to open and swallow me up, and there was nothing to do but smile and accept congratulations.

Even eleven-year-old Tommy's world revolved around the good news. There was still school and homework and choir and piano lessons and football and crafts and reading and stamp collecting and Scouting and fishing and Sunday School. But when he asked at the breakfast table, "What's today's date?" and, being told, ". . . The ninth," said, "Oh, boy! Just fifteen more days!" we didn't have to wonder what he was talking about. We knew he was counting the days until the baby's arrival.

The daddy of it all kept delighted too—except for the day when he overheard me talking to our neighbor about the need for a bassinet or a second crib. She and I had been discussing the complications of a two-story house, with all the bedrooms on the second floor, and how I'd find a second crib downstairs a real help during the day.

He heard just enough of the drift of the conversation to think I must have learned that we were going to have twins. For a moment, as he interrupted his conversation with the neighbor's husband and turned toward us, he didn't look like a proud papa at all. His face was pale and his knees were shaking. He looked like someone about to come down with a bad case of the flu, but he felt better after we cleared up the misunderstanding.

Surprised as I was at first, now that I'd gotten used to the idea, I couldn't imagine anything more wonderful and logical than that we should have another baby for the whole family.

God's promise of a new little life had overruled our foolish "wisdom" to the contrary and fulfilled the children's wishes. Having all been babies at once—Tommy, our oldest, was only four when Susan, our youngest, was born—none of the four could remember having a baby in our family.

When friends with babies would come to visit us I'd hear a

longing, "I wish we had a baby," from all of the children for days afterward. I hadn't paid much attention to their wishes, but apparently God had.

Feeling this baby was His idea, and not our own, we were confidently happy, not burdened with worry over the things that might have caused us concern—the German measles, the abdominal surgery, and other complications not uncommon when an "older woman" finds herself with child.

Until you've had the experience of expecting a new baby when you'd thought you'd already had your family, you can't appreciate the full meaning of the word "expecting." My suitcase was packed, the moon would be full tomorrow (even the scientific doctors believe that has something to do with the when of things), and a ready-made family was waiting to welcome the most "expected" baby of our lives.

10

The Waiting Game

WE WERE NOT the only ones expecting our baby. A magazine editor, planning to publish an article about our family, wrote to hurry me about sending pictures of the newest Harrell with its brothers and sisters. He apologized a little: "I realize how very, very busy you must be," he wrote, "but the pictures?"

I had to be apologetic too. "This is to let you know that I haven't been too busy to take the pictures," I wrote. "And I haven't been out of film. And the four older brothers and sisters have been willing to pose. But our 'expecting family' is *still* expecting!"

The new baby was overdue one week, two weeks, three weeks, four weeks . . .

My parents ran up quite a phone bill calling us long distance every few days, hoping to hear that something had happened. Their anxiety seemed to make the baby more determined to stay where it was.

One night the phone jangled us awake at 12:30 A.M. As my husband flew down the hall to answer it, the first thought that popped into my head was, "Oh! I'll bet Irene's had her baby!"

And I started down the hall to add my congratulations to the conversation.

The combination of cold floor on my bare feet and the ungainly shape in the mirror I passed straightened me out. *I was Irene*, and *I* was the one who was still "expecting!"

I was certainly as ready as I'd ever been.

The crib was in place in our bedroom upstairs. For daytime convenience there was a borrowed bassinet downstairs, loaned by a former baby-sitter. There were piles of lovely new baby things sent by Grandma and showered upon us by church groups and friends. There were boxes of not-quite-new but still good baby clothes from sisters and cousins.

I'd been wearing a maternity wardrobe composed of welcome leftovers from favorite friends. My hospital suitcase was freshly packed—again—except for the wristwatch of our youngest son. He wanted me to take it along so I'd know when it was time to feed the baby.

Expecting a fifth baby when we thought we were already a "complete family" had been different in many wonderful ways. Mama didn't get too fat because she knew it was important for her to stay healthy; Dad didn't get too flustered because he'd been through all this before; the kids were more excited than Christmas. With their hands frequently on my bulging midsection they had marvelled over every kick and hiccup. They'd reminded me of my iron pills, and had broadcast the happy news to everyone.

I suppose, if it had been our "first time around," we'd have worried ourselves to death and would be facing the approaching delivery with apprehension instead of joyous expectation. As it was, I thought often on Romans 8:28, taking it literally, several times a day: "And we know that all things work together for good to them that love God."

And so the great day finally came. December 30, 1964. Marguerite Owens Harrell, a squalling angel who should have arrived before Thanksgiving, entered fully into our lives. And they were never the same again.

11

Merry-Go-Round Miracle

AT FIRST WE didn't think anything was wrong. For months we believed our precious baby girl was as perfect as she looked. Tests at the hospital where she was born showed no imperfection. She was tiny, but complete. Her eyes responded to light, her heart sounded normal and her chest looked all right on the X-ray. And she was hungry all the time! On top of all that, her red hair was naturally curly. What more could anyone ask?

We weren't in the habit of asking for things anyway. Active members of a local church congregation by that time, we believed in God as the creator of all things and were sincerely thankful to Him for all our blessings. We prayed the Lord's Prayer, asking for daily bread, and forgiveness for our sins and deliverance from temptation. In a difficult situation we might even pray for guidance, but it never occurred to us to pray for healing, or for anything else calling for the direct intervention of God in the lives of men. We felt the power of prayer was invariably in what it did to the pray-er, not to the one prayed for.

And so we prayed our thankfulness for our baby and joyously took her home for the whole family to love and enjoy. We almost forgot that I'd had German measles during a time when the virus could have caused some defect in the baby. Our feeling at the time had been that God had already blessed us with four perfectly beautiful, normal children. If it was our turn to be entrusted with one who needed special care we ought to welcome the opportunity. We still felt that way. And we didn't worry about it.

As the weeks and months went by our little Marguerite grew dearer and dearer. Our lives were wonderfully enriched by this particular bit of heaven in our midst. We could not imagine how we ever got along without her.

And Marguerite was so good! For a long time we joked about her independence when she failed to look in our direction if we called her name. We called her a good baby when she slept through all the racket of our noisy household.

But after a while we began to wonder about her hearing. "Oh, you know her hearing is all right," a friend assured us. "Why, she jabbers and cries, doesn't she? And laughs? Deaf babies don't make any noises." She sounded so sure I didn't argue. I wanted her to be right.

One day I casually mentioned my wonderings to a pediatrician. He said, very matter-of-factly, "Don't think she hears well? Nonsense. Of course it's easy enough for you to tell. Just drop a heavy book behind her when she isn't looking. And see if she jumps. That'll tell you soon enough." But he didn't sound as if there was any urgency about it, so I let the matter rest.

I knew as little about deafness as my friend and the doctor. The first books I read on the subject were quite out-of-date. "If you think your child may be deaf," they said, "just try to be a good mother. There's nothing you can do about it until the child is old enough to go to school. Diagnosis of deafness is almost impossible until the child is four or five years old." I didn't know how wrong they were, nor how vital early diagnosis is to the well-being of a hearing-handicapped child.

So I kept wondering a little, but not too much, and continued to enjoy our baby. I wasn't ready to drop a heavy book or slam a door to find out the truth.

Then, one day, Marguerite was sitting in her stroller under the

carport when her daddy arrived home for lunch. Facing the back
yard she didn't see him drive up and come to a stop just a few
feet from her. He was ready to know the truth.

He blew the horn once, twice, three times. Then he stepped from
the car and slammed the door, hard. Calling to her in a loud voice,
her daddy walked right up to her stroller. 'Guerite did not turn, nor
change her happy expression, nor stop her babbling.

We knew then what we had been suspecting for several months.
Our perfect daughter couldn't hear a thing. Our baby was deaf.

When she was eleven months old we took her to the hearing
clinic at a large university. There the audiologist put us into a small,
thickly-carpeted room. Acoustic tile covered the walls and ceiling
so that loud noises would not disturb the rest of the building.
'Guerite explored her surroundings and played happily with toys,
completely unaware of the great variety of sounds introduced into
the room by a loudspeaker in the corner. Some of the sounds were
so intense that I wanted to cover my ears. But 'Guerite didn't notice
any of them.

"Profoundly deaf" is how the doctors classified her that day. "I'm
sorry," they told us. "Rubella deafness is, as far as we know, always 'nerve deafness,' not correctable by surgery—or any other
means."

Did we wish we had had an abortion to keep our child from
being born? Mercy, no! She was so bright and beautiful and happy,
a tremendous blessing to all who knew her. Would she ever wish
we had not let her be born just because she couldn't come with
a written guarantee of physical perfection? I couldn't imagine it.
God had managed to impart to us an overwhelming thankfulness
for this child—a thankfulness that left no room for tears about
her handicap.

One of our other children expressed it rather well, I thought.
One day, after playing with her baby sister, Susan came to me with
a look, half puzzled and half apologetic, on her face. She could
not know the full import of what she was about to say and she
knew it would sound cruel. What she said was, "Mama, I almost
don't feel sorry Marguerite's deaf, because there are so many other
wonders in her life." Although she might never express it in exactly

that way, we hoped and trusted that would be how 'Guerite would feel too.

When a special friend, learning that surgical correction of nerve deafness was not possible, lamented, "Then there's nothing that can be done," we had to contradict her.

"No," we told her, "*everything* has to be done." And we all began on the "everything."

The children took turns giving the baby "speech reading" opportunities, hoping she'd learn to understand us and eventually be able to talk intelligibly herself. I, who for years had been admonishing my children to be quiet and not talk so much, found myself encouraging them to be noisier all the time where the baby could watch them.

My husband and I enrolled for the correspondence course offered for parents of hearing-handicapped children by the John Tracy Clinic in California. Following the advice of a speech therapist we began collecting all sorts of noise-makers and duplicate pictures of objects and actions to use in teaching our baby.

Our reading headed in new directions. We borrowed books from the Clara Block Lending Library in Washington, D.C., in order to learn more about deafness. We read about how to help our child have a rich and full life in spite of her handicap. We subscribed to the *Volta Review*, the official journal of the Alexander Graham Bell Association for the Deaf, and joined one of their "Roundabouts," sharing our problems and solutions with other parents of deaf children.

We filled out application blanks to ensure our child's admission to the Eastern North Carolina School for the Deaf when she'd be old enough for kindergarten. The school was brand new and located in our own town!

We all whistled, sang, barked, jabbered, banged pots and pans with her, and turned the record player up loud. We did all the things supposed to be helpful in the auditory training of deaf babies.

Help and encouragement came from everywhere—North, East, South, and West. And help from on high? Did we ask for that?

Of course we continued to pray for our child—prayers of thankfulness. We were all so grateful for her that we couldn't even ask the blessing at mealtimes without adding a special P.S. of thanks for our darling 'Guerite. And we thought long about our favorite scripture, Romans 8:28: "We know that in everything God works for good with those who love him, who are called according to his purpose."

We could see so many ways in which God was working for good, even through 'Guerite's handicap. If every parent of a handicapped child had received as many blessings as we and our friends had through our Marguerite, the whole world would be clamoring to adopt handicapped children whose natural parents were unable to care for them.

While we prayed our thankfulness, others prayed too. Some of them prayed for her healing. We were too scientifically enlightened for that. Hadn't the doctors told us her deafness was not curable?

We didn't expect a miracle. We didn't even hope for one. Our daughter's deafness was a fact. We had accepted it completely. And we couldn't have loved her more or felt more blessed at being chosen to be her parents.

There were even advantages! Tommy had been wanting a woodworking outfit—a workbench with all that goes with it. We gave him one for Christmas, and installed it in the only available spot— in his bedroom, which was next to the baby's. Tommy hammered and sawed to his heart's content. I never had to say, "Be quiet, Marguerite's asleep." Turning a light off and on would wake her. Noises never did.

One day a saleswoman came to the door when 'Guerite was having a nap in the playpen in the middle of the family room. While the woman was showing me her merchandise, my own and neighborhood children banged in and out of the door, intent on their afterschool affairs.

When one began practicing noisily on the piano, the woman looked at me questioningly.

"Aren't you afraid they'll wake the baby?" she asked.

"Oh, no," I said, "noise doesn't bother her."

"Really?" she went on. "My baby wakes at the slightest sound. It's so aggravating. I'd give anything if she'd sleep like that!"

Oh, no, you wouldn't, I said to myself as she repacked her samples. *You wouldn't at all. You see, my child is deaf.*

I didn't say the words aloud, just smiled and changed the subject. I didn't want to break her heart. People didn't always understand that it was all right.

But our church friends understood—especially the praying ones. One had put her arm around me a few days before our first visit to the hearing clinic.

"About your appointment with the audiologist," she said, "everything's going to be all right, isn't it?" It wasn't really a question the way she said it. It was an affirmation of faith.

"It already is all right," I told her. "It already is." Neither of us meant that 'Guerite could hear. It was just that God had made her deafness all right for her and for us to bear.

But then something started to happen. We first noticed it on Christmas Day, right before 'Guerite's first birthday. She had learned to make a little kissing, smacking noise with her lips— small wonder, she had been kissed so much. But the marvel of it was that when I made the same sound behind her back she turned to look at me and laughed. I tried it again. It worked every time —even when she didn't know I was behind her until I made the smacking noise. 'Guerite was hearing something!

In the days that followed she began reacting to other sounds too—not all sounds, just some few like a shrill whistle, a loud handclap, a banging together of pots and pans. When I excitedly reported this to the audiologists they cautioned me against being too optimistic. "No, it doesn't mean that she's actually hearing any better," they said, "just that she's responding to the auditory training you've been giving her. Keep up the good work."

They had to be wrong. I couldn't believe that our "good work" had caused the significant changes in 'Guerite's response to sound. Soon I no longer needed to tap my foot on the floor to get her attention. I could shout her name and she'd look up at me.

In March, four months after our first visit to the hearing clinic, we took 'Guerite back for additional testing. The doctors had a hard time believing what they saw and heard. The jabbering our baby was doing didn't sound like the jabbering of a deaf baby. It had too much inflection and range for that. And, in the little acoustically treated room, instead of failing to respond to sounds of 110-decibel intensities, as she had on our first visit, 'Guerite was obviously reacting to some sounds of only fifty decibels.

Our "profoundly deaf" daughter was now merely "moderately to severely hard of hearing." That would still mean a hearing aid and special speech therapy, but she might even be able to attend a regular public school with hearing children!

The scientific explanation for what had happened was something the doctors were not sure about. They suggested hers might be a case of "slow maturation" or unusual "autism." But neither of those was borne out by other aspects of her development. The doctors had never seen a case like hers and were frankly puzzled.

As I stood listening to their conjectures about what might have happened to our child, I began to wonder. Whatever the scientific terminology for it, wasn't the real explanation "prayers and miracles"? But I didn't ask that out loud. And I didn't answer it even to myself.

One of our church friends had accompanied us to the clinic that day. I called others as soon as we got home. One had kept our other children at her home after school. She rejoiced at the wonderful news.

Emily hadn't been able to go with us or to keep our children. She had only prayed. It was hardest of all to tell Emily what we had learned. I don't remember how I said it, but all the telephone heard was the intermingling of our tears. Together we shed the tears none of us had shed before.

In that moment my tears acknowledged what my lips had not. A miracle *had* happened to our baby—a miracle straight from God. And the miracle was surely wrought because Christian friends who loved her had prayed for just such a miracle.

Marguerite was deaf. Now she could hear. It *was* already all right, above all we could ask or think or dream! But not above all that our friends could pray for. Not above all that a precious child could receive from the grace of God.

The next Saturday Emily came to see us. She carried with her a big bright yellow package and placed it before 'Guerite, who was in her high chair, finishing up her lunch. Opening the package,

'Guerite squealed with pleasure as she pulled out a beautiful little merry-go-round.

"How perfectly darling," I said, and turned to thank my friend.

"No, wait a minute," Emily whispered and reached out to wind the pink knob on top. I wondered at the wetness of her eyes and the tremulousness of the smile shining through. But then I understood.

As she released the knob, the merry-go-round horses began to dance and I heard the soft tinkling of lilting merry-go-round music. With her gift Emily was telling us that she had faith that this child who was deaf, who could now hear very loud noises, would someday delight in this fragile melody.

How could I not believe in intercessory prayer after all that had happened? How could I not join my friend in praying for a merry-go-round miracle? It wasn't too much to believe any more. Nothing was.

Nothing would ever be too much to believe again. God, working through our prayers, *can* heal even "incurable" afflictions.

What does that mean for our lives? Far more than our joy at 'Guerite's ever growing response to the world of sound. It means that the miracle of prayer is an everyday thing for us now, embracing every aspect of our lives, reaching out to bless all our friends. We can pray for ourselves, for them, and for all the helpless, the hopeless, the "incurable." And we can tell them so.

Every day we see what prayer can do.

Yesterday 'Guerite heard the merry-go-round.

12

Too Much Togetherness

"BUT, MAMA, I didn't eat the soap!" Aware that four-year-old Alice was taking a long time in the bathroom, I had opened the door to check on her. Her irresistibly innocent defense emerged from the middle of an unbelievable mess.

The washbasin was overflowing, brimming with sodden towels and washrags; the contents of the wastebasket floated and sank in the toilet; the floor was a puddle, strewn with toothbrushes between the carefully laid toilet paper paths; and little green toothpaste worms squiggled everywhere. Eating the soap must have been what Alice was planning to do next. She had already done everything else.

But why? Why was my precious daughter turning into a house-and-harmony-wrecking creature? She unwittingly gave me a clue a few weeks later when I surprised her too late to prevent another catastrophe, one that mere cleaning up couldn't undo.

That day I discovered a small mound of glossy brown hair in the middle of the rug. The pitiful-looking creature playing beside it was Alice's little sister. A gleam of forbidden scissors disappearing behind Alice's back made it unnecessary to ask who the culprit was. Too heartbroken at the sight of my two-year-old's scarecrow haircut to be angry, I had pleaded, "But why, Alice, why? What on earth made you ruin Susan's hair?"

Alice had shrugged her shoulders and replied, matter-of-factly, "Well, I just didn't have anything else to do."

I should have realized, way back then, that something was wrong with the way we were raising our children—that maybe we weren't giving each one enough individual attention, encouraging each in activities suitable for his age and inclinations. But I didn't.

With four children in our cheaper-by-the-dozen brood by the time the oldest was four, I quite naturally adopted every timesaving method that worked. I was proud of my efficiency, and blind to its real results.

I treated the children like identical products on an assembly line. When one was fussy for a nap, I put the whole crew to bed. When I went shopping, I returned home with four identical treats. When I called, "Time to get up!" or, "Time to go out and play!" I meant for everyone to hop to it.

And yet they weren't quadruplets. They weren't even as alike in temperament, ability, and interests as you would usually expect brothers and sisters to be. But I was too busy to notice. Handling them all as one unit seemed to make sense.

Almost from the time the baby was big enough to be bathed in the bathtub, I dumped them all in at once. I'd wash all the faces, then, with soap on my washrag, all the necks and ears, arms, and the rest of it. If one came out looking redder than usual, another a little dingy around the fringes, it was probably because they had shifted positions in the tub when I wasn't looking and one had gotten a double scrubbing.

After pajamas were donned their daddy usually got in on the act, telling them to line up for their vitamins. They were so cute, lying side by side on the living room rug with their mouths open like so many hungry baby robins in a nest.

Daddy used one bottle of vitamins and one dropper for all. He was germ-conscious, careful not to let the dropper touch their lips, but it didn't occur to him, or to me, to wonder whether the same dosage was, in fact, appropriate for all of them.

Home life is supposed to be better than institutional sameness, but who could feel special under our system? Treated as a unit, with total togetherness, they were bound to misbehave. Stifled individuality erupted in behavior problems.

We'd been having trouble with the oldest boy. He was always wandering off without permission. I wouldn't have let him go to a friend's house if he'd asked me, since they couldn't all go. And I found things in his pockets when I was doing the laundry—things like marbles, and rubber bands, and once a little cap gun. Ordinarily the mother of a six-year-old boy wouldn't be surprised at the presence of such paraphernalia in her son's pockets. I was, though, because he wasn't allowed to have any of those things— they'd be dangerous to the baby.

Was it surprising that he borrowed the treasures from a little friend and accepted them "for keeps" when they were only loaned for an afternoon's playtime? It shouldn't have been. This same child was forever disappointing me by being undependable. Small wonder, since we kept treating him like a baby. Where was the motivation for him to act grown up?

But we didn't ask ourselves that question. We kept on making the same mistakes, and others as well.

There was the matter of allowances. From the beginning we gave the same weekly allowance to each child. Kites, model airplanes, glue, and all the special things a primary child needed kept our oldest boy broke. The baby didn't know anything to buy with her money, so her savings account began to look like college insurance right away.

And there were chores. We didn't begin assigning daily chores until the youngest child was old enough to make her own bed. Then everyone had chores—making beds, emptying wastebaskets, shaking rugs, clearing the table, folding clothes, and the unending "cleaning out their junk." We rotated the jobs, so no one could feel he was being treated unfairly. I marvel now that the "it's not my turn" wailing didn't start sooner.

We required the same standards of achievement from all of them. Many times the youngest fought back tears of frustration as she struggled to make her bed as smooth as the others had theirs.

Because the children were all together all the time, there was no peace. I had to do more settling of disputes than a professional labor arbitrator. Still vivid in my memory, because it happened so often, is the sight of three-year-old James scrambling out of the sand pile and up the steps to the screen door to report, "Mama, Tommy hit me."

I'd go flying out to administer whatever discipline seemed appropriate, or ignore the bickering if I thought the neighbors' eardrums could stand it. Of course the kids fought all the time— they were apart from one another only for punishment. Sometimes I think they welcomed "solitary confinement." Maybe they were even naughty on purpose. It should have been clear for a long time that my "efficiency" was multiplying our problems rather than reducing our work.

You'll be happy to know that we finally woke up. But it took a new baby to straighten us out. With her coming, when the youngest of the older children was already seven years old, identical treatment for all was, temporarily at least, out of the question.

Baby had to be treated differently. Somehow the concrete fact that someone had to have a different bedtime, that someone had no chores, that someone couldn't do everything the rest did, was the stimulus we needed to start undoing some of the togetherness at our house.

Baby is over two years old now, and we're no longer stuck with the same allowance for everybody. We recognize that the expenses of Scouting and school lunches ought to make a difference. I'm not afraid to require more chores from the older children or to expect a higher standard of performance from them. They no longer go everywhere together, because we let their natural interests express themselves. Someone goes to piano lessons while another goes to Scouts. One takes handicrafts while another builds a tree house. There are fewer cries of, "It's not fair!" because they no longer expect to be treated all alike.

Encouraging individuality means I have fewer disputes to arbitrate and the children are better friends when they are together because it's no longer all the time. Togetherness is richer all around when it is not the perpetual order of things.

I'm enjoying the children more. The kids are not only happier, they're more interesting. Did you know that one is a whiz at math? He can work in his head some problems I'd need a lot of time and paper to figure out. And another, whose math is the despair of his teacher, is a talented creative writer. And the one who got scalped long ago is an artist of great originality. And the one who didn't have anything else to do has more successful projects under way than I could dream up in ten years.

I no longer merely love my children, I love Tommy, Alice, James, Susan, and Marguerite—all the separateness of each of them, and each as if he were the only one. That's the kind of security they needed all along.

That our new approach is undoing some of our former problems is evident, too. A few days ago, as I commended the oldest for the fine way in which he'd completed a particular task, without supervision, he gave me a good summation of the whole business: "Well, Mom, it kind of seems like you've started treating me like I was older than the rest of the kids. And that just automatically makes me feel more trustworthy."

Oh, we still see remnants of overdone togetherness; that's natural since we had them at it so long. But my eight-year-old's letter to Santa last year was a real milestone of the progress we've made. Her letter wasn't a request for four identical bicycles, as it was a few years ago. This time she enumerated the different things each child wanted, asked Santa to remember the poor children, thanked him, signed her name, and added a P.S.: "So, Santa, you might just as well bring one of everything." That she asked for one of everything, instead of five of each, was proof to me that we're finally on the right track.

13

Every Child Should Be an Only Child—Once in a While

EVERY CHILD should be an only child—once in a while. I know that's not what the psychologists are always telling us, but I found out the practical truth of it last summer quite accidentally.

The house seemed strangely quiet and empty one Monday morning. Tommy was away at Boy Scout camp; Alice and Susan were spending the week with friends in another town. The baby was having her morning nap and my husband had gone to the office for the day. James and I stood in the kitchen and just looked at one another for a minute.

I confess I was feeling a little bit sorry for him, stuck at home with me while everyone else was getting to do something interesting. As we were clearing the table and putting the pitifully small load of breakfast dishes in the dishwater I learned that he didn't need my sympathy.

"Know sumpin', Mama?" he confided. "This is gonna be the best week of my life!"

"Why, what do you mean, James?" I asked him, quite puzzled

at his unmistakably cheerful outlook.

"Well," he replied, "this week, when you ask me to do something, I won't have to wonder why you didn't ask one of the other kids to do it instead."

James was as good as his word. He enjoyed being my exclusive, indispensable, right-hand man and eagerly performed many tasks, accomplishing helpful things without even being asked. I didn't hear a single complaint. He acted as if doing chores for me was his favorite activity.

With the other children gone I had time and patience for letting him help with special undertakings. We spent a whole afternoon making cookies for the freezer. That's an occupation that gets a little bit fussy when everyone tries to help; it leaves us all worn out and cross with each other. But with just one helper it was a relaxed measuring, sifting, mixing, and baking session. James and I had lots of talking and listening time for each other. No one got lost in a big family shuffle.

At the end of the week, when we were all reunited at home again, each child told about what a good time he had had. And it sounded to all of us as if stay-at-home James had had the best time of all!

A month later Alice was at church camp and James was in Chapel Hill, spending a few days with his cousins there. Tommy and Susan were left at home and I was holding my breath. Sibling rivalry—to use the polite word for it—had frequently been rampant between those two. Much to my surprise they became real buddies that week. They worked together, played together, conspired together to surprise me with breakfast in bed one morning, and, in general, thoroughly delighted in one another's company. I needn't have felt sorry for them, either.

When I asked Susan how they had managed to bury the hatchet so effectively, she explained, matter-of-factly, "Well, with everyone else gone, we just couldn't afford to fight. Then we wouldn't have had anybody to play with!"

Apparently the week had given those two an important opportunity to need one another, a prime requisite for getting along peaceably together. Friendly remnants of their happy week together are still visible in their relationship. I was beginning to understand that larger than average families could build togetherness by using a few blocks of "apartness" occasionally.

We found other advantages for us as parents, too, in letting the children spend time apart. Having a smaller family some weeks we got better acquainted with each child and experienced the unique dearness of each one of them at his best. Too often, before, we had had to give attention to the one who showed a clamant need for it, and had undoubtedly missed some of the sweetest parts of parenthood.

The vacation from sibling bickering was almost too wonderful to believe. It was so restful to let one child talk all he wanted instead of having to shush him to let someone else speak. I didn't have anyone to scold about interruptions.

Our annual trip to Ohio to visit grandparents gave us another summer chance to divide the children and conquer family friction. We took full advantage of it. To keep from imposing all seven of us on one household we let some of the children stay with cousins who lived nearby. I started to apologize to the one who had to stay with me at Grandma's but what he said stopped me.

Looking at the makeshift bed fixed for him on the davenport, Tommy exhaled wearily and happily. "Gee, but that's a comfortable place to sleep!" he murmured as he crawled in, nearly asleep already and so contented he was almost purring. "I sure am having a good time here at Grandma's with you and Grandpa and Daddy," he volunteered. The absence of young playmates hadn't bothered him a bit, and getting to stay up later than usual and participate in a couple of strictly grown-up fishing trips had made his "only child" days perfect.

I had discovered the advantages of five "only child" children during the summer. With the coming of fall I thought, at first, that I'd have to wait until next summer to enjoy "only child" children again. But a little thinking and some slight maneuvering showed that we'd not have to wait at all. There are lots of ways to reap "only child" benefits all along—to "keep your five and have one, too."

Almost every afternoon lately my eleven-year-old daughter has come home from school and headed for the kitchen to help begin

preparations for supper. I'm letting her do most of the cooking because it's something she wants to do. I've decided that she's not
suddenly that crazy about KP, but is unconsciously taking advantage of her best chance to be an "only child" while the others
are out playing. She can tell me privately about her day as we
work together over recipes she's compiling for her own cookbook.
We can discuss her problems and interests and she can ask questions without the others interfering. Our mother-daughter relationship is thickening, along with the pudding she stirs.

Friends have been helpful, too. Some of our best friends love
children, and have already seen their own grow up and move far
from home. When I let one of mine spend the afternoon with one
of the left-alone mamas, everyone benefits. The friend enjoys my
child for company, my child enjoys "only child" attention, the
children left alone get along better with one another, and each one's
slice of my tender-loving-care is larger.

"Only child" treatment can be quite simple. It can take the form
of taking one child on a special shopping trip, one child to the library to pick out books to read, one child to the doctor for a
check-up.

Even days home from school with childhood ailments are perfect
opportunities to administer all-important exclusive treatment. Convalescence is ideal for listening to Mama read aloud or for enjoying
personalized party frills on a luncheon tray for the two of you.

Reading these suggestions over my shoulder, Susan said, "Well,
Mama, it can be even easier than that! Sometimes I like it when
just you or Daddy are in the room with me, even if the other kids
are downstairs somewhere." And I'm sure Susan's right.

Each child needs all of our attention some of the time. Occasional
exclusiveness makes both parents and children more appreciative
of one another and better fitted for harmonious family living. And
it's relatively easy to arrange "only child" treatment for your house-
ful once you make up your mind to do it.

An "only child" is so special I'm glad we have five of them.
And, now that I've discovered the sense of it, I plan to enjoy my
five "only child" children more frequently and more fully from
now on.

14

TV or Not TV?

Is it possible to rear normal children in today's world without a TV in your home? We think the answer is a resounding "Yes!"

Recently a friend complained to me, "Sometimes I wish TV had never been invented!" She was exasperated. Her efforts to control her children's television viewing were frustrated by the prevalence of poor programs, worse commercials, and general bad taste. There were few hours when the TV set could be trusted to provide wholesome entertainment or helpful learning experiences for her family.

Of course she wasn't planning to take the television set out of her home or to turn it off for good. But she was almost hoping that it would break down and stay that way for a few days. Then she would have some respite from making and enforcing decisions about what her children could see.

Many conscientious parents are like my friend. They acknowledge that the presence of a TV set in their homes is not an unmixed blessing. But they don't seriously consider living without one.

Instead, they attempt to keep some measure of control over their children's viewing. They may require school homework and household chores to be completed before the set is turned on. They may limit total hours of viewing and encourage plenty of outdoor exercise. They may make certain programs "off limits" to keep their children from seeing constant violence, sex, sadism, divorce, and tragedy.

Sometimes their control is effective; often it is not. Frequently its most obvious result is the opening of a new area of parent-child friction in their lives.

We have never had a television set in our home. In the beginning, TV or not TV was decided for us. We simply couldn't afford one. Now, five children later, we are deliberately without a television set even though we might be able to squeeze TV payments into the budget. I will admit that it takes "some doing" to avoid succumbing to the constant pressures and temptations to buy one.

The last of our periodic re-evaluations of our TV decision centered around the children's responses to the question, "Should we or shouldn't we get a TV set?" As is so often the case, they mentioned things more pertinent and significant than the ones that occurred to us.

Ten-year-old James wants a TV because other children occasionally make fun of him for not having one. According to him, they go around chanting, "James doesn't have a TV!" When this kind of reasoning crops up, I know I haven't done a good job of teaching him that conformity isn't the best thing in the world. Being different is necessary for the kind of specialization our civilization requires. A good time to forestall a "keeping up with the Joneses" attitude with its attendant miseries of budget-breaking certainties is now.

James's desire for a TV set has another prop. In his words, "Besides, people like the Three Stooges have been silly for so long they've probably got the habit of it. If nobody had a TV set I bet they'd starve because they couldn't do something else like maybe work in a filling station or something like that."

While I appreciate and encourage compassion in my children, I think I can rechannel that bit of it into something a little more necessary. We'll let someone else worry about how the Three Stooges will pay their grocery bills if TV entertainment folds.

Nine-year-old Susan wants a TV so that when she's sick and has to stay indoors she can watch cartoons and Westerns all day. She has done so little TV viewing that she thinks there would be some program appropriate for her at every hour. As it is, when she has to stay indoors she spends much of her time in art work. She has completed pictures for a children's book that will surely find a publisher. No TV-glued convalescent could boast of such an accomplishment.

She thinks too that a TV would help her entertain her little friends when they come to visit. Lacking this easy alternative, they play games, school, read to each other, or just sit and giggle—all of which, to my mind, are infinitely preferable to sitting absorbing whatever the omnipotent eye has to offer.

Susan says, "I know another reason too. If you just had two or three no-good toys, you'd see something on TV that you'd like to have. Then you could go to the store and buy it."

She's surely right about that. At least that's what advertisers count on. TV would stimulate her little "gimmes" far beyond the possibility or advisability of her gettings.

"And one more, Mama. TV makes people happy, and it would make us happy."

Would it? I wonder if anyone has calculated just how much unhappiness TV spreads by bringing into little lives the woes of the world—woes they can neither understand nor remedy.

Alice likes a little variety in her days. She said, "Well, on rainy days, Monopoly, cards, Scrabble, making cookies, cleaning out my junk, reading, embroidering, drawing, playing the piano, and working on my stamp collection get monotonous. When it's raining and you don't have any friends around, TV wouldn't be the same thing over and over."

You've been watching it—is the fare on rainy afternoons what would ordinarily be good for a sweet young girl?

Giving me an indisputable TV advantage, Alice went on, "We need a TV to be informed about what's going on. When they launch rockets I don't know much about it—just what I read in the paper. When the kids at school say 'Did you see so and so on TV last night?' I just have to listen."

Maybe that's the secret of Alice's popularity. Everyone loves an interested listener. And couldn't we arrange to see the few things every year that are considered "essential television" without bringing the total TV problem into our lives? I think it would be worth a try.

Thirteen-year-old Tommy is my extremist, usually. He had a vehement answer ready. "Don't want one. Just don't. It would take up my time. It costs money. If someone gave us one I still wouldn't want it. I wouldn't be able to do Scout things and my homework. I'd be a weakling. I wouldn't read enough. I'd get too lazy and fat. You have to have something to eat when you're watching it. I wouldn't get my exercise."

Mercy! Tom talked as if the TV would be a personal enemy, making him do things he didn't want to do—as if he wouldn't have the willpower to withstand its attractions. I'm afraid he might be right—for several of us.

Listening intently to Tom's outpouring, James was halfway inclined to agree with him. "Mama, some people think I'm great because I don't have a TV," he said. "They say, 'Gee, James can live without a TV!' Like it makes me bigger or braver than they are or something." Apparently he does realize that difference has its desirable aspects, after all.

"Besides," he continued, "then we wouldn't learn some of the things they show. And we wouldn't hear some of the ugly talk, or learn to set forest fires and strangle people."

I had to shiver at that. But isn't he right? Haven't the crime commissions decided that excessive viewing of TV violence is directly responsible for many crimes actually committed?

Alice piped up with some negative reactions too. "If we had a TV, we'd probably like the Beatles!" Here she stopped and made motions of washing her mouth out with soap.

Isn't there a little sanity in children who regard "Beatle" as a bad word? In boys who never let their hair get long deliberately? In girls who gag instead of swoon when they see a hip-swinging Elvis Presley preview? There's joy for their parents, all right, in children who hum a theme from *Liebestraum* or *Finlandia* or the *Peer Gynt Suite* instead of apeing blatant, tasteless, singing commercials. As a taste-former TV seems to scrape bottom too often for me.

After all these opinions had been expressed, it seemed a good time to ask a further question. "Suppose," I began, "suppose all our debts were paid and we had five hundred dollars to spend on something. Would you like to have a nice new color TV or something else?"

I held my breath, but I needn't have bothered. The priority lists they gave me put everything from a screened-in porch, an organ, clothes for the baby, camping equipment, more books, a farm, a pony, a workshop, and a fish pond ahead of their desire for a TV set. It's plain that TV or not TV for our family is settled for several years and some thousands of dollars to come.

Our conference had lasted two hours. But it was worth it. The time had passed so quickly with all interested in the thinking and sharing that had been going on. When I shooed the kids to bed, thanking them for their opinions, they went up the stairs reluctantly. They had enjoyed my listening as much as I had enjoyed their talking.

And I heard James muttering on his way up, "And another thing not good about TV—it takes up talking time."

As so often happens, a postscript contained the most important part of the message. How often does your limited family time together turn into a joint TV viewing session of something mediocre instead of a precious opportunity for you to share and grow together? Hours of real communication are rare and vital, not profitably supplanted by anything else, however "educational" it might be.

We know we make many mistakes in the rearing of our children, but, at the moment, "no TV" doesn't seem to us to be one of the mistakes. "TV or not TV?" is an important question. The answer doesn't have to be automatic acceptance. We can't settle it for any family except ours. You'll have to do it for yours.

15

Seeing Stars

"HEY, MOM, I've found a new star!" James, with his freckled face and cowlicky red hair, made an unusual looking astronomer. He was breathless with excitement as he burst through the kitchen door and thrust a handful of thorny blackberry briars at me.

"Wait a minute," I cautioned, backing away from the thorns and putting down the onion I was peeling. When I had wiped away the onion tears with the back of my hand I took a look at him. There were ugly scratches on his arms and a big rip in his good school shirt. But my sigh of annoyance was lost in his tumble of words.

"Tommy and I were cutting a path back to our camp in the woods. We were just putting the briars in a pile when I happened to see that the end of one of them made a star. And it wasn't just *that* one—all the briars had stars where we cut them, even the old dried up ones! Do you see 'em, Mom? There are zillions of stars right in the briar patch!" James finally stopped to take an enormous breath.

He was right, I discovered, as I gingerly examined the briars. The cross section of each of them formed a perfect star. The tender briars had a pithy white star in the center, outlined by the delicate green star of the outer covering. Older stalks were hollow brown stars that let the light through when I held them up to the sun.

We'd never noticed stars in briars before. No wonder James was excited. I was too. I even forgot to scold him for wearing a good shirt on Saturday and offered him a cookie instead. He'd have been too excited to eat the cookie if he'd known about the stars we were to discover a few minutes later. But let me tell you about some of the others first.

Seeing stars has been one of the favorite hobbies at our house for several years. I don't remember how we came to discover the first one. I may have been slicing apples for some cinnamon apple rings when I recognized the beautiful star formed by the pattern of seeds in the apple. To me, it was a reminder of the Star of Bethlehem which pointed the Wise Men to the place where the young child lay. And it was a kitchen reminder of the direction in which I should point my life.

The Wise Men followed the star, and stars have been following us ever since. Our family and friends have had stars revealed to them in many places—in the seed patterns, blossoms, stems, and fruits of a number of growing things—in pears, oranges, pine cones, roses, sunflowers, tomatoes, squash, lettuce—there is even a star within a star within a star folded in the heart of the lowly cabbage. It's as if God has planted the star of the heavens in the fruit of the land to help us keep Him in our hearts.

Not many weeks have passed without adding a new star to our collection. The star in a bunch of celery was revealed the day a friend came to tell us the doctors had pronounced her cured of cancer. The exquisite, unmistakable, double star in the cap of a strawberry was revealed to me only after I had capped nearly a hundred pints of them for the freezer.

I wondered why it took me so long to see the strawberry star. Because it is always there. Was it that I was blind to the star until I knew it must be present?

In his wonderful *Of the Imitation of Christ* Thomas à Kempis observed, "If only your heart were right, then every created thing

would be to you a mirror of life and a book of holy teaching."
When my heart is right, then only am I able to see His purpose in
everything. And it's not always easy to see His purpose in the
tragedies of our lives. Most of the time we just have to have faith
that it is there, even though it may be concealed from our eyes.

When he had finished his cookie and drained the last quart of
milk I dabbed at his scratches with some iodine. We talked about
God's stars and their meaning for us and agreed that there must
really be stars in everything He made. Anywhere we had not discovered them yet we just hadn't looked with a right heart.

Then James picked up a briar to take upstairs to show his sisters. It happened to have five smaller branches forking from it.
You know what he found when he looked along the main stalk
toward the branches. They made a star too.

And then James looked at me. "You don't suppose—you don't
suppose that even the *thorns* make a star, do you, Mama?" I
considered a minute before I dared to look.

Why not? I thought. In my own life, disappointment, pain, and
sorrow had invariably proved to have God's purpose for me en-
graved upon them. In our marriage, problems had provided
avenues for growth. But I always had to get a little distance away
from adversities to realize that. I had to view them with a right
heart to see how they fitted into God's purpose for my life.

Could it be the same way with thorns on blackberry briars?
Could it be that when I backed off a little from the prickling and
pain of them that they would make stars too—symbolic of God's
purpose in our troubles?

My hand shook a little as I picked up the greenest of the briars
and sighted along it. James knew the answer without my having
to tell him. My tears—not onion tears this time—told him that
the thorns didn't grow from the briar in just any old way. They
grew only from the star ridges. Their pattern formed star after
star after star as far as the briar grew.

We didn't ask, "Could it be?" or, "Do you suppose?" We knew,
without consulting any botanical encyclopedia, that the crown of
thorns with which they mocked Him was a crown of stars leading
us to worship at His feet.

16

Mama's Free-lancing—
A Family Affair

"How on earth can you write with all those kids?" My friend,
all wrapped up in her only child, viewed our five progeny as a
surely insurmountable obstacle to the free-lancing career at which
I kept hopefully plugging away.

"How can I write with 'em?" I rejoined. "Why, I couldn't write
without 'em!" My reaction must have sounded more than a little
bit bristly and protesting, but she seemed not to notice.

"Really?" she asked. "You mean the kids actually *help* you with
your writing? But all that laundry, and the cooking, and the cleaning, and the homework, and—"

Her sputtering incredulity almost made me doubt the truth of
what I'd said. A big family does mean lots of work. But it means
lots of living, too. The longer I thought about it, the surer I became that our five children have been indispensable ingredients in
all my attempts to put words on paper for profit.

Almost any writer would acknowledge that there are little
mechanical things that kids can take care of for them. These little

chores help keep them happy with Mom's career by making them a part of it. I never have to sharpen my own pencils, chew the erasers, make paper-clip chains, lick stamps, count the number of words in a manuscript or interleave carbon paper with erasable bond and yellow second sheets. The children are glad to keep those things done for me.

And any writer with children knows he won't lack sympathy and support when the inevitable rejection slips arrive. The children's indignation at these frequent outrages helps a lot.

"You mean they didn't buy your story?" The question is followed by snorts of disbelief and then by eloquent defense: "Your story's a whole lot better than those other stupid things they publish. I bet they'll be sorry when it gets to be a best seller!" Who can be discouraged with a cheering section like that?

Ideas at low ebb? The kids are always brimming with them. One day I was stumped by a writing assignment for a correspondence course. I had to write a story about a picture. The picture showed a policeman and a small boy sitting in a diner. There was a red kerchief bundle on the floor beside the boy. I thought he had probably run away from home—but why?

When I asked my own little boy to help me out he looked at the picture for a long minute. Then he said, "I don't think he's running away at all. Maybe he's just going to see his grandma."

That was it. James had solved my problem and the assignment practically wrote itself. Later, when I got a check for "The Runaway," James and I shared it.

Ideas for writing frequently come from questions the children ask me. Our eight-year-old artist had drawn a picture of a man. He was fat, dressed in blue overalls, and had a bald head with a small dark fringe of hair above his ears. Susan wanted us to name him for her. "Oscar Peabody" was the unanimous choice.

Then she had another question. "What do you think Oscar Peabody does for a living?" There was no question about it. Oscar just *had* to be the proprietor of an old-fashioned general store.

We couldn't leave it there. A character as interesting looking as Oscar literally begged to have a story written about him. *No Doughnuts for Breakfast* hasn't found a publisher yet, but it will.

My eldest was captivated by Joan of Arc when he read a library book about her. Ever since, Tommy's been nagging at me to add St. Joan to the list of saints I've interpreted for young people. I know I'll do a chapter about her, someday.

Ideas the kids give me deliberately are helpful. So are the ones they supplied before any of us thought I'd have a writing career. The children began to help it along before it ever began!

I used to take time to write to their grandparents frequently, telling in great detail all the funny and naughty things they did and said. Grandmother, bless her, enjoyed the letters and saved them to return to me. They're full of wonderful things I would have forgotten, things that provide the perfect spice for articles in the form of anecdotes and inimitably authentic small-fry conversations. Insights worded as only childhood innocence can frame them have triggered more than one devotional article for me.

And problems? Kids keep you plentifully supplied with those, too. Much of what I have written is personal stuff, designed to help someone solve intelligently problem areas we managed to flounder through. Solutions that occurred to us somewhat tardily might be helpful to other families. "Too Much Togetherness" and "Getting It Done," both purchased by *Home Life,* are examples of articles born from our problems with the children.

When Alice was a first grader she had a quarrel with one of her little friends. Encouraged to think about her anger in a constructive, Christian way, she was able to forgive her friend and to make an overture that healed the broken relationship. Seeing the practical application of forgiveness she wrote the first draft of what became "Patty Finds The Way" for *One/Two.*

Children can give professional editing help, too. If you don't believe it, give your completed article to an intelligent grade-schooler to read aloud. Does it really say what you meant to convey? Are the sentences easy to read? Does it hold the child's interest? Material that doesn't read aloud well isn't going to impress an editor with its clarity.

I'll have to warn you about being sincere when you ask for editing help from your children. I made a mistake there once and had to retype an article as a result.

Alice was only six when I asked her to read the final copy of a children's story all ready to mail. I was an even poorer typist then than I am now and to have achieved a perfect copy of a two-line poem would have been something. This particular three-page manuscript fairly gleamed with perfection. And that was before I had discovered erasable bond, too.

I had Alice wash her hands first and cautioned her about rumpling the paper in any way. Instructing her to read the perfect copy to see if there were any mistakes in it, I left the room for a few minutes. When I returned she said, "It's mostly all right, Mama. Just the places I have marked are wrong, is all."

Marked! Mutilated, she should have said! Great heavy pencil marks from her dark black first-grade pencil hid several lines on each perfect page. And they weren't there because of any typographical errors. "I just thought it would sound better if you said it this way, Mama," she explained.

Can kids actually be helpful to an aspiring writer mother? All the way from sharpening pencils to painful editorial suggestions. And what better proof do I need than this book itself? Without the kids, I couldn't have written it.

17

Schedules for Family Living

I HAVEN'T always thought I'd like schedules for family living. Pretending that we were all free to do pretty much as we liked, I didn't keep an orderly written-down account of things we were supposed to do.

I don't remember what the so-called advantages of my unsystematic approach were, but I can clearly recall, and shudder at, the hectic, nerve-wracking frustrations of it.

We all regularly forgot important dates we wanted to remember. I had to nag, nag, nag at the kids to get them to do their piano practicing, to do their chores, to finish their homework—even to get out and play in the fresh air!

Long-planned vacation trips found me frantically rushing around at the last minute trying to get clothes mended and ironed for the suitcase packing. Sunday mornings before church were always particularly hard to survive. There'd be forgotten white shirts to iron for the boys, dessert to prepare for the company dinner, and housecleaning to be finished that should have been done days before.

Ridiculous? Of course. But I didn't figure out exactly what was wrong, nor what could be done to correct it, until we were forced to make room for one more activity in our busy lives. That came on a day when it was clear, even to me, that hard-to-decipher reminders on little scraps of paper (that usually got lost in the shuffle) and my less than elephantine memory would have to be supplanted by something a little more reliable.

I was sitting in the doctor's office where my son James had just finished going through all the complex tests of an allergy clinic. Our pediatrician had sent us to find out the cause of James's distressing asthmatic symptoms.

The allergist told me that I would have to take James to the clinic twice every week for desensitization shots. I swallowed hard, but figured I'd work them in somehow. Our household of seven kept me quite busy already.

Then the allergist said to my son, "Now, James, you'll have to do your breathing exercises twice every day—without fail."

James didn't even blink, but I must have groaned aloud. The doctor looked at me strangely, and I had to explain that I was really all right. But the thought of one more thing about which to remind James every day had momentarily almost made a patient out of me.

"Mama won't have to remind you about your breathing exercises, James," the doctor assured his young patient. "You *do* want to get well, and the exercises are important for you. Just put them down on your daily schedule and let it remember for you." James nodded, as if he already *had* a schedule to live by.

And, much to my surprise, when we got home that day he started making one. He adapted the little schedule blank in the front of his school notebook and made an extra copy to hang on the wall beside his bed.

I was delighted to discover, a few days later, that James was actually living by it. That's why I had been finding his bed neatly made every morning. It was included on his schedule.

James had allotted a certain time every day for his piano practice, his Scout work, his household chores, his breathing exercises, his school day, his taking care of his baby sister after school, and even his play time! My nagging at him hit a new low. Even his music teacher noticed a difference, because James no longer forgot to practice every day.

That's when I began to wonder if schedules for all the rest of us might make sense too. It was worth a try.

The first thing I did was to sit down and write out a tentative daily schedule for myself for a whole week in advance. It was immediately clear where some of my trouble spots were—and *why* they were trouble spots. I had, for example, left too many essential things to be done on Sunday morning. Shifting some of them to Friday and Saturday really eased that first weekend for me.

Inviting the rest of the family to make out individual schedules for themselves uncovered other mistakes. Reviewing the schedules they made, I saw that I had been requiring entirely too many chores of my oldest daughter, barely leaving her time to breathe. I couldn't blame her for complaining sometimes. That was something I could correct right away.

Some of the children were aware that too much of their free time was really wasted. Susan decided to schedule half an hour of drawing or painting for herself every day. The growing gallery on the wall of her room gives her a sense of accomplishment and worth.

Each child scheduled his fun as well as his work. That made their schedules look far more inviting. It made them aware that they did have a lot of free time. I think that looking at the schedules of their parents gave them a better appreciation of what we do for them, too.

Individual schedules helped a lot, but they weren't all we needed. We had to have a larger, all-family master schedule as well. That was necessary to make sure we didn't have irreconcilable conflicts.

I bought a large desk-blotter-size calendar from the stationery store and hung it, with pencil firmly attached, on the wall beside our telephone. We don't enter everything on the master calendar, just things that involve anyone's being away from home or having guests here.

I don't discard last month's calendar page when I take it down at the end of the month. I fold it and file it in my desk instead. The old calendar pages are helpful in more ways than one.

They're a record of the children's ailments and doctor visits, for one thing. And, when I'm feeling discouraged about never seeming to accomplish anything, I can look back and have a better idea of where my time went. That information has helped me mend my ways when that's what was required to improve the fabric of our lives. And the calendar occasionally cheers me up with its authoritative, "You did *too* accomplish something last month—just look!"

Now that we have schedules for everybody we're getting things done we never supposed were possible before. I've actually caught up on my mending! That never happened until I began to schedule a weekly half hour for it. It's such a relief to know that the clothes hanging in the closets are actually ready to wear, not merely waiting for "emergency repairs" when we don't have anything else left to put on.

My twelve-year-old daughter has taught herself touch typing, just because she put a half-hour block on her daily schedule for that and stuck to it. Tommy may get his God and Country award in Scouting after all, if he continues to follow his schedule with his present enthusiasm.

And my busy lawyer husband lives up to his promise of three nights a week at home with his family, because that is on the schedule too. He put it there himself, since he knows it's important. Ordinary meetings and invitations don't lure him away.

Our change from a life of frantic forgetting to one of scheduled serenity isn't complete, but we can see where we're heading at last. And there have been fringe benefits we didn't foresee, too.

There's greater family harmony when inevitable schedule conflicts are spotted early, while there's still time to make changes or work out acceptable compromises. "First come, first served" is a helpful calendaring rule, one that encourages all of us to keep the master calendar up to date.

Realizing the benefits of scheduled living, we've begun to make order out of some of the other chaotic areas of our lives. A written record is mightier than a mere string around a finger to remind us of errands to be done, letters to be written, or things to be picked up at the grocery store. We're learning the economies of fewer shopping trips now that our current list is a permanent fixture in the righthand corner of our master calendar.

Scheduling things intelligently and writing them down does far more than save time, money, and tempers. Surprisingly enough, instead of feeling tied to a schedule, we find ourselves freed by it —freed from the nagging and the forgetting and the combination of underachievement and overexertion of our old haphazard regime. Although we made our schedules firm we kept them flexible, knowing they were designed to help us, not to hinder or frustrate.

Most important of all, scheduling automatically makes us put first things first, where they ought to be, not accidentally crowded out altogether as used to happen so often.

So let it be written, so let it be done.

18

Sex and Stuff

BEFORE BEGINNING this chapter I thought I'd do a little research. I didn't have to go to the library for the kind of research I had in mind, just to the attic where there were some dusty old boxes of letters I had written to Allen and he had written to me before we were married. I thought they might tell me what kind of persons we were and what thoughts we shared with one another as we contemplated marriage.

Mercy! I learned a lot all right—some of the letters made me blush. It's a good thing we did marry—there was blackmail material galore! It was obvious that, among other things, we were most awfully in love.

I assume that most people *are* in love—or suppose themselves to be—when they decide to marry. It's a good thing. Love conquers all, they tell me, and there's a lot to conquer when two people begin living together as husband and wife.

Just think of all the awful cooking that grooms have to survive in the beginning! My new husband had to eat hard fried eggs for months before I learned how to cook them soft the way he likes them. And the mashed potatoes always turned to cement before the meat was tender. I don't remember that he ever complained. He might not even have noticed. Love conquers a lot.

It *has* to.

When I wrote my publisher, hinting that I might like to do a book on marriage, he seemed to think it was a good idea. "I have looked at some marriage manuscripts recently," he wrote, "but most of them lack honesty and reality, or are overburdened with romanticism. . . . Could you do a chapter on the marriage bed with candor and common sense? This would be very helpful."

I'm sure it would. Before I was married I read all such chapters I could find. None of them were very helpful. And they were invariably embarrassing. They were all so clinical, so automatic, like a series of pushbuttons (with anatomical labels) you should manipulate to achieve a desired effect. They treated sex as a physical thing—and it's so much more!

Now, after fifteen years of married life, five babies, and one miscarriage, I am still distressed by most marriage-bed chapters. I'm not Victorian or prudish, just practical. The more they try to tell all, the less they succeed in conveying what sex is all about. Their minute descriptions are like autopsies, performed on dead objects. And sex is a *living* thing!

Now it may be that everyone needs to read a few sex books in order to satisfy his adolescent curiosity safely, to understand the nature of his own body. But successful sex in marriage isn't acquired by a study of technique or anatomy. It's acquired by growth in loving, in giving to, in wanting to please the person for whom you've forsaken all others.

Way back when I was in high school I went through a stage when I couldn't have gone to sleep at night without reading a chapter in my Bible and reciting (I didn't know how to pray it) the Lord's Prayer. I don't think these rituals did much for my soul's growth, but I performed them regularly.

After I was married, I was likely to do my Bible reading—if at all—at some other time of the day than bedtime. Sex and religion were in two entirely different compartments of my life. I just couldn't go from reading the Bible to kissing my husband goodnight—I mean, really.

Well, I'm years older now, and far wiser. I'm married to a whole lot more than my husband's body. I'm married to his mind and soul as well. Our love is no longer a compartmented thing, with physical love in one place and spiritual and mental sharing in another. We love with our whole selves. When we're most nearly one with Him in a spiritual sense we're most able to be perfectly one in a physical sense as well.

The world would have given up the search for interesting aphrodisiacs a long time ago if it had discovered the richness of relationships in a Christian marriage where fidelity and a mutual seeking after God are pursued and lifted up. Sexual harmony is not to be found for the seeking of it for itself. It is a by-product of seeking first the kingdom of God. And it is a harmony above all we could ask or think.   *Eph. 3:20*

Of course you won't learn that just by my saying it. You might even think I'm being sacrilegious. You'll have to experience it for yourselves in order to believe it. My publisher might even think I'm being unrealistic or not quite honest. But I'm not.

The gift of physical love comes from God. He doesn't blush when we do, talking about it. And He surely didn't make sex a thing to be ashamed of. It's only our misuse of it that makes it shameful.

Think of the billions of people in the world. They all got here *that* way. And there's always been a lot more of *that* going on than there are new people to show for it. Sex must be more than merely permissible, it must be one of the most wonderful earthly gifts of God. He made sex pleasurable on purpose!

That doesn't mean that, in the modern world, sex relationships are automatically problem-free. It doesn't mean that honeymoon sex is at all comparable to the experience of husbands and wives who've lived together for years, becoming more and more one person in their total lives and responses.

Live and learn? Remember the first dress you ever sewed or the first biscuits you ever made? Ugh! Yes, live and learn. Love and learn, too.

But suppose that sex just isn't working for you—that practice, instead of making perfect, is making life increasingly unsatisfactory and unsatisfying. Maybe you need to see a doctor or talk to a marriage counselor. Don't be afraid. They won't be embarrassed by your questions, your problems, or your anatomy. Counselors hear lots of questions, cope with a lot of problems, and doctors see a lot of anatomy every day. It's as common to them as dirty dishes are to you. And they may be able to help with advice, counseling, or simple surgery, freeing you for a fuller expression of your love.

Chances are you don't need any of that. It may be enough to seek to grow more loving, to seek to please your spouse (*especially* when you don't feel like it). The rewards may surprise you. Sometimes it's in the midst of unselfish giving that we receive the most, when we're not seeking to receive at all.

Well, love is fine—marriages can't *live* without it. That's generally agreed. But there's something else too, something that's not so generally realized: liking is important, and so is believing in the same things.

Allen and I liked each other. He was someone I could respect, someone I could look up to. In one letter I wrote: "I love you for what you believe. There's not an ounce of opportunism or compromise in you. You're real, and I marvel at my getting a chance to be your wife. . . . Marrying you is a betrayal of none of the things I really believe in. One of the many wonderful things that I love about you is the charity with which you understand and look past faults in others—so that you can believe in them for something, and your belief in them makes them better people."

Before our engagement I wanted Allen to come to Ohio to meet my family and visit with my friends. I wanted to be with him in cold Yankee daylight and see if he was as wonderful as he seemed to me to be in romantic Chapel Hill.

He passed the test—I won't say he passed it beautifully, because he'd worn his least becoming suit on the plane and his luggage was missent to Washington, leaving him in the same unattractive brown suit for most of a wrinkled weekend. But the suit couldn't have mattered less when I took him to meet one of my best friends.

A few minutes after our arrival at her house all four of her small children were swarming over Allen like so many excited puppy dogs. And he was actually enthusiastic about their affection.

That did it. I knew I'd always like him anywhere. And there'd never been any doubt in my mind about the love part of it.

Liking a person is *so* important. We err when we assume that liking automatically and invariably accompanies physical attraction.

A woman in Newcastle, England, recognized the difference. The unmarried mother of four illegitimates explained her failure to marry their father, saying, "I don't like him enough." I imagine many girls have dated boys they might "love" in private but couldn't "like" in public.

Liking, between marriage partners, has to include respect for one another. By nature a rather overbearing, bossy know-it-all, I had to be taught to let my husband run his own life.

Not many months after our marriage one of Allen's brothers came to see us. During the evening he took a cigar from his pocket and handed another in Allen's direction. I opened my mouth and was surprised to hear myself say, "Oh, Allen doesn't want to smoke that. He's trying to cut down."

All my husband said—bless him—was, "Thanks, I believe I will."

The look he gave me was not one a woman would ordinarily cherish, but I do. The look cured me. So did the smoke from the four (or was it five?) additional cigars he smoked that night. There was no danger I'd ever be a bossy wife again, even inadvertently.

Any woman who has been trained not to be bossy owes a great debt to the one who broke her. Can a marriage be truly happy where a wife is permitted to boss her husband? I doubt it.

Back during the second World War we heard a lot about priority lists. Steel was needed for the war effort, and war needs had top priority. We couldn't buy a bathtub until my father's doctor certified that he needed a tub for his health (he really did). Then the government gave us the right to buy a tub. We came first, we had priority over other people who wanted a tub merely for the sake of convenience.

Building materials came under priority rulings too. We lived on a farm and needed building material to construct sheds to shelter the ewes during lambing season in the chilly spring. The official to whom my father talked didn't know much about the farming business. He suggested that instead of building the shelter my father should postpone the lambing season to more clement weather!

I don't remember whether we ever got the priorities for the building material or not, but these two incidents made an indelible impression on my mind.

What do priorities have to do with a good marriage? A lot.

A good marriage is important to me. It's one of the things I hold most dear. It's a whole lot more important to me than many other things I would also like to have. I put a happy marriage at the top of my mental priority list. And I try to remember to live accordingly.

A written priority list might be helpful to you in attaining or preserving a happy marriage. Begin by making a list of the things you want. Be sure to list the trivial along with the vital things. Put the items down just any old way at first. Your list might look like this:

> THINGS I'D LIKE TO HAVE:
> my own way
> a mink coat
> a happy marriage
> no ashes on the rug
> a vacation at the beach
> hollandaise sauce on the asparagus
> sheets tucked in at the foot of the bed

Then after you've made your list—and it might go on for pages and pages—recopy it, putting the most important item at the top, the next most important second and so on down to the thing you care least about.

You'll recognize right away that some of the items are incompatible. Your husband can't stand sheets tucked in at the foot of the bed. So which do you want most—a happy marriage or tucked-in sheets? You can't have them both. Maybe if you were all of six feet two, tucked-in sheets would bother you as well. So don't tuck them in; they don't have top priority. Sure it takes a little longer to get the bed made in the morning cause the sheet is all whopper-jawed. But so what. You know what you wanted most and you're getting it.

And a happy marriage is such a wonderful thing, it's worth giving up a lot more than tucked-in sheets. You can even see yourself giving up the hollandaise sauce if he gets mad every time he sees it. (Besides, you can always have that when you're shopping by yourself and have to stop in a restaurant for a bite of lunch. Or, the night he eats with his lodge.)

No ashes on the rug would be nice to have, but he smokes, doesn't he? That automatically means ashes on the rug, unless you nag and fuss about it and then there'll be ashes anyway and both of you will be upset. So quit mentioning it. Quit thinking about it. And don't even sweep the ashes up when he's around. That'd be calling his attention to it and he'd take it as a personal criticism. Get the ashes up when he's not there to be annoyed by the vacuum cleaner. Or just leave them for a few days. What if that visitor thinks you're a sloppy housekeeper? That's just fine. She keeps a neat house. There are no ashes on her rug. Her husband doesn't live there any more, either. How would you like that?

You can keep your mouth happily shut about a lot of things because you really do love being happily married. It's one of the wonders of the age. He loves you! and it's mutual.

You might even have something about sex on your priority list. Maybe you're not interested in lovemaking on Friday night after you've had your hair done. But the stuff the girl put on your hair makes you smell "come hither" as all get out. Your poor husband gets a whiff, gets all interested and bothered in spite of himself, and then what?

Which would you rather have? A happy marriage or an unruffled coiffure? Both? That's probably not possible without a little more forethought. Better decide which you really want most. You're likely to get your way. I imagine more than one marriage has been sacrificed for a hairdo. Sometimes they're mutually exclusive. Next week maybe you can try being extra amorous on Thursday and be able to keep your hairdo *and* your marriage on Friday.

After you think about all this for a while you can dispense with a written priority list. You'll know and behave automatically as if a happy marriage is worth all you ever have to give up for it.

And now, we come to the most important thing of all.

19

Crack-Up

Most folks who knew us wouldn't have guessed we needed a miracle. We were in good health and possessed of all our faculties. Happily married for fifteen years, we had been blessed with five beautiful children. We had lots of friends, a comfortable home, and an abundance of blessings that money can't buy. Although our budget was usually a little strained, we always had enough to eat and to wear. When we needed it, the bank loaned us money without collateral.

All seven of us went to church every Sunday. My husband and I taught an adult Sunday School class and worked on the evangelism committee. Allen, my husband, was an elder and had recently finished a term as chairman of the board. Embarrassingly often we were held up as an example of a fine Christian family.

Because of Allen's position as city judge we counseled lots of people in trouble—people in trouble with alcohol or in-laws or spouses or children or neighbors or the law. We listened unendingly, patiently and lovingly, and talked to them about how God loved them and could help them with their problems if they would let Him.

Both of us made religious talks in other churches or at meetings. At our house there was always a blessing at mealtimes. I was writing articles for religious magazines and had just had my first book published. *Prayerables* was the name of it, and its purpose was to make people more aware of the presence of God in their lives.

Everybody thought we were of the "elect"—not in money or social position, but in the rightness of our lives.

They couldn't have been more wrong.

It was only to those out of earshot or out of seeing distance that we were perfect.

Inwardly? Mercy! Only God knew, and we were living as if He didn't exist.

I don't know how He could stand to be around that summer. Days dawned bright and beautifully or breathtakingly fragile with morning mists. Quail and mourning doves made an early symphony in the woods and fields below our house.

But there was nothing beautiful about me.

By nine-thirty every morning I'd be snarling at the children. Everyone was so cross and contrary I didn't know how I could possibly survive through the summer.

The older children brought out the evil in me with their incessant bickering and general laziness. I even found myself getting angry with our precious baby.

'Guerite at two and a half was the most beautiful child imaginable, with dark slate eyes, a delectable complexion, and curly red hair that positively glowed. Because she didn't hear well, she wasn't able to talk much yet. Her wants were mostly expressed in terms of a pointing finger with an accompanying, "Anh, anh, anh," and a tugging at my hand or skirt to get my attention.

Any reasonable mother, blessed with such a lovely child, would have dried the dishwater off her hands, or turned the iron off until naptime, or let the vacuuming wait until 'Guerite was happily occupied.

But I wasn't a reasonable mother. I had a lot of work to do and woe unto anyone who got in the way! Several times I was on the verge of shaking my darling from aggravation at her wordless frustration.

The whole summer had been hectic and full of emergencies. "Vacation" was only six weeks old and we'd already had one case of pneumonia, one hernia operation and appendectomy, six stitches in a knee, eight in an injured ear, one serious kidney infection, one twelve-hundred-mile trip to visit grandparents, and an over-productive garden with more blackberries, corn, beans, tomatoes, squash, peppers, beets, cucumbers, grapes, and asparagus to be harvested, shucked, frozen, shelled, sliced, canned, preserved, jellied, jammed, pickled, and juiced than Del Monte ever dreamed of. The telephone rang every ten minutes, the doorbell nearly as often, and hordes of neighborhood youngsters made themselves at home, bringing tons of junk on permanent loan, and leaving muddy sneaker tracks, strewn Monopoly sets, dirty drinking glasses, spilled sugar and paper doll scraps in their wake.

But the worst was yet to come. A baby robin, lost from its nest, found its way to our doorstep. Sounds simple? You've never fed a baby robin for long. It took all of the time of all of the children and all of their friends to dig worms enough to keep him alive.

Added to their already full catalogue of excuses for not doing their work was a new one.

"But Mama, I've *got* to find some worms to feed Chirp! You don't want our baby robin to die, do you?"

They looked accusingly at me, suspecting what I'd answer if I were truly honest, as I grimly hosed bird droppings off the carport steps for the umpteenth time and re-laundered the sheets on the line *again*.

I kept fretting about my desk, piled high and higher each day in my study where I'd had no chance to sit down for weeks. There were two book deadlines looming September first, and numerous articles waiting to be written.

To top it all off, my husband's secretary went on vacation. His law practice had been in the doldrums, but that week there was practice galore. There were deeds, wills, complaints, answers, and writs of habeas corpus for me to type—in triplicate, with accompanying affidavits—in my "spare" time.

I remember telling the kids menacingly, and my husband apologetically, "I'm on the verge of cracking up!"

Only God knew how right I was, and what the words really meant. Well, no, I take that back. I suppose the devil had an inkling, too, and was hoping the crash would throw me irrevocably in his direction. I was certainly headed there, and was assuredly mean enough, and full enough of hates and despisings and frustrations to have served him superbly.

I was actually looking forward to the inevitability of a nervous breakdown. The thought of being a pampered patient in a hospital—even a bedlam mental hospital—appealed to me. There'd be no pressure on me then. Someone else could tend to all the "Mama, this," and "Mama, that." Someone else could find the lost shoes or the misplaced library book. Someone else could wash and iron and cook and clean and entertain and worry about the kids' quarrels. Someone else could listen, listen, listen.

Well, I did crack up. I did break down. Only it wasn't at all like I supposed it would be. It was a miracle. It was the best thing that could have happened to me. It was the freeing of my life from all the unendurable pressures upon it.

No lights flashed. No bells rang. No men in white coats came to get me. There wasn't even a burning bush. But I was changed. It wasn't so much that I saw God as that I acknowledged His looking at me.

Let me tell it, as much as I am able.

It was night. The children were in bed and Allen and I had flopped down to read a little before going up ourselves. He was reading some Peter Marshall sermons and I had Catherine Marshall's *Beyond Ourselves*.

The pressures of the summer had made me most awfully aware of my tremendous shortcomings as a mother, a wife, a neighbor, a friend, a Christian. I couldn't have been more receptive to what Catherine Marshall had to say.

Usually, when Allen and I are reading together, we interrupt occasionally to share something we find. We weren't doing it that night. I could tell, from the way Allen would lean his head back and close his eyes and from the set of his mouth, that he was being mightily stirred by what he was reading. I wiped a little dampness from my cheeks now and then.

I read the chapter "How to Enter In." Catherine Marshall told how she had found Christ and made a commitment of her whole life to Him. And how a drunk had done the same thing. And even a minister had been led to a new knowledge of and commitment to Him who alone matters in all of our lives.

Catherine Marshall didn't ask, "Don't you want to get on your knees and surrender?" If she had made one move in my direction I'd have run the other way. She didn't ask, she didn't even suggest. She just witnessed to what He had been in her life and in the lives of other people.

Oh, that was what I needed too! That was what I had to have!

I handed the book to Allen and asked him to read the chapter. He knew from my face that he had to do it right then. That it was something tremendous.

I ran upstairs and knelt at the foot of our bed. Now that might not strike you as an unusual thing for a Christian woman to do, but it was unusual for me. I had always done my praying in silence, sitting up, and it was only mildly confessional, not heart-rending and soul-stirring-up.

This was different.

I was still on my knees when Allen finished the chapter and came up to join me. And he's a slow reader.

I told Allen what I wanted to do with my life, that I wanted to give all of it to God. And then I asked, "Is it the right time for you?"

I didn't want to pressure or crowd him in any way, but I wanted so much for us to be together in this, the greatest thing that had ever happened to me. It *was* the right time, and he knelt beside me, and we prayed together.

We'd never really prayed together before, not confessional giving-up-our-fractured-lives-and-wills prayers. Neither of us had ever made a *total* commitment of our lives to God, and Catherine Marshall's book had made us realize it. We'd never before been sufficiently aware of our own lostness to let Him find us, to be saved. We were that night.

We've prayed together, out loud, on our knees, every night since. And we don't ever intend to stop. And, instead of rolling over

when the alarm rings and burrowing under the covers for an extra
forty winks, we get up, extra early, to have time to begin the day
with half an hour of "holy" reading, meditation, and prayer.

What a difference it makes!

The litany in church that Sunday morning was almost too much
to bear, it was so personal to us:

"Out of my distress I called on the Lord; the Lord answered
me and set me free.

"I thank thee that thou hast answered me and hast become my
salvation."

I had a new life! And Allen had one too. We were new Chris-
tians, committed entirely to Christ. Our problems and responsibilities were His. We were merely administrators, carrying out His
will as it was revealed to us. Our *very lives* were not our own. They
were His.

The children saw the difference in us right away. But that will
be another book. It's all part of a continuing miracle, now that
"I" have cracked up, and He has taken His rightful place in this
life I used to call mine.

the beginning